D1611000

THE BIG BOOK OF
Cigarette Lighters

IDENTIFICATION & VALUES

JAMES FLANAGAN

COLLECTOR BOOKS
A Division of Schroeder Publishing Co., Inc.

Front Cover: King Case, pg 56. Johnson Wax Tower, pg 25.
Evening Purse, pg 32. Elephant, pg 21. Popeye, pg 83.

Cover Design • Beth Summers   Book Design • Erica Weise
Cover Photography • Charles R. Lynch

Collector Books

P.O. Box 3009
Paducah, Kentucky 42002-3009
www.collectorbooks.com

Copyright © 2005 James Flanagan

Searching For A Publisher?

We are always looking for people knowledgeable within their fields. If you feel
that there is a real need for a book on your collectible subject and have a large
comprehensive collection, contact Collector Books.

Contents

Dedication

Once again, I dedicate this book to my best friend and loving wife, Patricia.

Acknowlegments

To my wife, Patricia, for the long and countless hours spent helping from the beginning to the end of this project. Her patience, understanding, and encouragement made this project possible.

To my wonderful children, Teresa, Lisa, and Jimmy, for their support and for spending countless hours at shows and antique shops with me looking for lighters for my collection.

To my father, Melvin Flanagan, for always being on the lookout, wherever he is, for lighters to add to my collection.

To my mother, Marie Bowser, for all the lighters she has given me.

To Judy Reilly and my wife, Patricia, for the many hours spent photographing the lighters and accessories so beautifully.

To everyone at Collector Books Publishing Company for their interest and help in making this book possible.

To all the people and friends that I have met at the antique shows, shops, and through the lighter clubs.

Introduction

Welcome to the *Big Book of Cigarette Lighters*. Creating this book has been a labor of love as collecting cigarette lighters has become more than a hobby for me, it has become a passion. The pages of this book are filled with many wonderful kinds of lighters, as I have tried to present a truly comprehensive book of lighters from many different manufacturers and eras. Many of the names in this publication you will recognize, such as Evans, Ronson, Lennox, and Zippo, while other names like Supreme, Hamilton, and Imaco may be less familiar to you. Some operate with electricity, some are battery operated, and some are fluid and flint, or butane. There are many different shapes and sizes from the 1800s to the present time. Essentially, there is something for everyone.

For all of the lighters and accessories pictured in the book, there is a complete description, with dimensions and values. This book is a must have for the seasoned collector because it encompasses so many different kinds of lighters and because it contains the latest price values. For the new collector, this book will show you how vast in scope this hobby has become. You may notice that values can differ greatly from publication to publication, however I feel the values put on the lighters in this book are accurate. Of course, I am looking through the eyes of a collector, not a dealer!

So, as you get ready to thumb through the chapters of this book, I thank you for choosing the *Big Book of Cigarette Lighters* and I hope you will enjoy reading this book as much as I have enjoyed putting it together.

Advertising

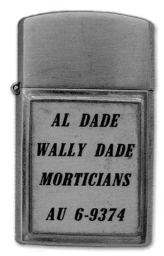

Chromium lighter with advertisement decal on front, made by My-Lite. Circa mid 1960s. 2¼"h, 1½"w. **$5.00 – 15.00.**

Chromium advertising pocket lighter for funeral director, made by Warco. Circa early 1960s. 2¼"h, 1⅛"w. **$10.00 – 15.00.**

Both tube style chromium and enamel pocket lighters, made by Redilite. Circa late 1940s. 3"h, ⅜"dia. **$20.00 – 30.00 each.**

Replica of 1932 chromium Zippo pocket lighter in a gift box. Circa 1988. 2½"h, 1½" w. **$25.00 – 35.00.**

Chromium pocket lighter, made by Lansing. Circa 1975. 1¾"h, 2"w. **$10.00 – 20.00.**

Large Lucky Strike chromium and painted table lighter made in Japan. Circa late 1950s. 4⅜"h, 3"w. **$30.00 – 40.00.**

Chromium and enamel pocket lighter, made in Japan. Circa 1955. 1¾"h, 2"w. **$15.00 – 20.00.**

Butane lighter in holder. "Denver Police Union" printed on holder, made by Big Pen Corp. Circa 1978. 3⅝"h, 2"w. **$5.00 – 15.00.**

Brass pocket lighter with gift box, made by Evans. Circa late 1930s. 2"h, 1½"w. **$25.00 – 40.00.**

Brass pocket lighter with the "Fraternal Order Of Eagle" on the front, made by Hurricane. Circa 1940s. 2¼"h, 1½"w. **$20.00 – 30.00.**

Advertising

Chromium and painted pocket lighter, made by Penguin. Circa late 1950s. 1¾"h, 2"w. **$15.00 – 20.00.**

Chromium table lighter, made by Bowers Mfg. Co. (showing advertisement on side). Circa late 1940s. 3½"h, 1¾"w. **$25.00 – 30.00.**

(a) Metal bottle-shaped lighter, painted red, with an ad for Lutz Lounge, made in Canada. Circa mid 1950s. 3¼"h, ½" dia. **$15.00 – 20.00.** (b) Coor's beer plastic bowling pin. Made by KEM. Circa early 1950s. 2⅞"h, ⅞" dia. **$20.00 – 25.00.** (c) Guinness metal beer bottle. Made in Ireland. Circa mid 1960s. 2½"h, ¾" dia. **$15.00 – 20.00.**

"Venetian" slim chromium pocket lighter by Zippo. Circa 1992. 2¼"h, 1¼"w. **$20.00 – 30.00.**

Chromium and enamel pocket lighter, made by BARLOW. Circa 1965. 2¼"h, 1½"w. **$10.00 – 20.00.**

Plastic butane pocket lighter, made in Korea. Circa 1985. 3"h, 1"w. **$5.00 – 10.00.**

"Typhoon" pocket lighter by Ronson with an engraving of a concrete truck done by hand. Circa mid 1960s. 2¼"h, 1½"w. **$20.00 – 30.00.**

Both chromium and enamel tube style pocket lighters, made by Redilite. Circa late 1940s. 3"h, ⅜"dia. **$20.00 – 30.00 each.**

Red Bakelite oil drum with an ad for Dodge Trucks. Circa 1940s. 3"h, 1¾" base dia. **$15.00 – 30.00.**

Painted metal table lighter that holds a disposable butane pocket lighter. Circa early 1970s. 3½"h, 1¾"dia. **$10.00 – 20.00.**

Advertising

"Willie" the Kool penguin table lighter, made of painted metal. Circa mid 1930s. 4"h, 1½" dia. at base. **$100.00 – 125.00.**

Chromium pocket lighter, made by SUN. Circa mid 1950s. 2"h, 1½"w. **$10.00 – 20.00.**

Alpine and Philip Morris cigarette advertising pocket lighters, made in Japan. Circa 1960s. Both 2"h, 1⅜"w. **$15.00 – 20.00 each.**

Chromium pocket lighter, made by Penguin. Circa early 1960s. 1¾"h, 2"w. **$15.00 – 25.00.**

1935 Varga Girl in pewter on a chromium finish Zippo lighter in a tin gift box. Circa 1993. 2¼"h, 1½"w. **$40.00 – 50.00.**

Chromium and painted tube style pocket lighter, made in Japan. Circa mid 1950s. 3⅛"h, ⅜"dia. **$20.00 – 30.00.**

Zippo anniversary series 1932 – 1992 chromium pocket lighters with tin gift box. Also came with six lapel pins. Circa 1993. 2¼"h, 1½"w. **$95.00 – 120.00 for the set.**

Chromium pocket lighter with decals on the front and back, made in Japan. Circa late 1960s. 2¼"h, 1½"w. **$5.00 – 10.00.**

Rosen–Nesor pocket lighter with "Lake Shore Club of Chicago" and emblem, with box. Circa 1950s. 1¾"h, 2⅛"w. **$15.00 – 25.00.**

Chromium and enamel painted pocket lighters. (a) Ad for bank in Denver Colorado. (b) Public Service of Oklahoma. (c) Winston cigarettes. All made in Japan. All circa 1960s. 1¾"h, 2⅛"w. **$10.00 – 20.00 each.**

Advertising

Brass table lighter with a pull chain mechanism. Has an eagle on top of the world with a banner saying "GMAC Plan." Circa 1935. 3¼"h, 2⅛" dia. at base. **$25.00 – 40.00.**

Metal oil drum for ZEP cleaner. Circa 1950s. 2¼"h, 1¼" dia. **$15.00 – 25.00.**

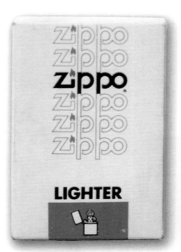

Chromium and enamel pocket lighter, made in Japan. Circa 1965. 1¾"h, 2"w. **$15.00 – 25.00.**

Chromium promotional pocket lighter for Mack Truck, by Zippo, in a gift box. Circa 1976. 2¼"h, 1½"w. **$25.00 – 35.00.**

Marlboro cigarettes promotional brass lighter, by Zippo, in a gift box. Circa 1991. 2¼"h, 1½"w. **$25.00 – 35.00.**

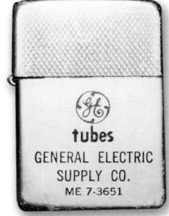

Brass and enamel pocket lighter, made by Park Industries. Circa late 1950s. 2¼"h, 1½"w. **$15.00 – 25.00.**

Camel promotional cigarette lighter in a gift box, by Zippo. Circa 1993. 2¼"h, 1½"w. **$25.00 – 35.00.**

Chromium and enamel pocket lighter, by Vulcan. Circa mid 1960s. 1¾"h, 2"w. **$20.00 – 30.00.**

Bottle pocket lighters. (a) Black & White. 2½"h, ¾" dia. (b) Johnny Walker. 2⅜"h, ⅝" dia. (c) Vat 69. 2¼"h, ¾" dia. All circa early 1960s. **$15.00 – 25.00 each.**

Glass bottles with metal caps. (a) Tribune Vermouth. Circa late 1950s. 5¼"h, 1⅜" dia. **$15.00 – 25.00.** (b) Canadian Ale. Circa late 1950s. 5 "h, 1⅛" dia. **$15.00 – 25.00.**

Advertising

Chromium pocket lighter with decals on front and back, made in Japan. Circa early 1960s. 2¼"h, 1½"w. **$20.00 – 30.00.**

Plastic Coca-Cola bottles with metal caps. Could be used as pocket or table lighters. Circa 1953. 2½"h, ¾" dia. **$25.00 – 40.00 each.**

Chromium and enamel slim pocket lighter, made by Park Lighter Co. Circa mid 1960s. 2¼"h, 1"w. **$15.00 – 25.00.**

Chromium and enamel pocket lighter, made by Barlow. Circa early 1960s. 2¼"h, 1½"w. **$15.00 – 20.00.**

Small table or pocket lighter of a ship for "Swedish Chicago Line," chromium and paint, by Sarome. Circa mid 1960s. 1⅛"h, 3¼"w. **$20.00 – 30.00.**

Brushed chromium pocket lighter with old concrete mixer truck, in chromium. Made for Walt Flanagan & Co. by Zippo. Circa 1986. 2¼"h, 1½"w. **$25.00 – 35.00.**

Chromium pocket lighter, made by Zippo. Circa 1963. 2¼"h, 1¼"w. **$15.00 – 25.00.**

Concrete advertising lighter for Walt Flanagan & Co., in brushed chromium, made by Rite Point. Circa 1960. 2¼"h, 1½"w. **$25.00 – 40.00.**

Replica 1932 lighter with a service kit containing fluid, flint, cleaning brush, and tweezers, in a gift box, made by Zippo. Circa 1990. 2¼"h, 1½"w. **$25.00 – 35.00.**

Chromium 60th anniversary (1932 – 1992) pocket lighter, in a tin gift box, made by Zippo. Circa 1992. 2¼"h, 1½"w. **$30.00 – 40.00.**

Advertising

"Bosch of Germany" spark plug lighter, in chromium and paint. Circa 1975. 3¼"h, ⅞" dia. **$25.00 – 40.00.**

"International Lighter Collectors Seventh Annual Convention" brass lighter, by Zippo, with a wooden box. Circa 1993. 2¼"h, 1½"w. **$30.00 – 40.00.**

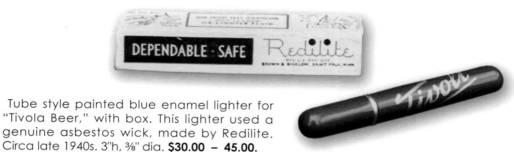

Tube style painted blue enamel lighter for "Tivola Beer," with box. This lighter used a genuine asbestos wick, made by Redilite. Circa late 1940s. 3"h, ⅜" dia. **$30.00 – 45.00.**

Animals

Brown painted metal Scottie dog, made by Strikalite. Circa late 1930s. 2½"h, 3"w. **$25.00 – 40.00.**

White painted metal Scottie dog, made by Strikalite. Circa late 1930s. 2½"h, 3"w. **$25.00 – 40.00.**

Black painted metal Scottie dog, made by Strikalite. Circa late 1930s. 2½"h, 3"w. **$25.00 – 40.00.**

Brass wolf (dressed as a cowboy) striker lighter. Circa mid 1930s. 5½"h, 2"w. **$275.00 – 325.00.**

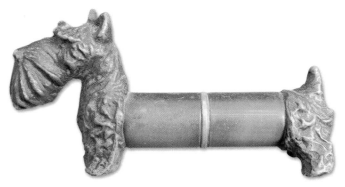

Brass Scottie dog lighter, made in the USA. Circa mid 1930s. 1⅝"h, 3¼"w. **$100.00 – 125.00.**

Butane chromium table lighter of a horse, made in Japan. Circa 1988. 7"h, 4½"w. **$20.00 – 30.00.**

Metal kangaroo, made in Japan. Circa late 1960s. 3¾"h, 3½"w. **$15.00 – 20.00.**

Animals

Sliverplate and enamel table lighter from the 1933 Chicago Worlds Fair (lighter located under dome on camel's back). 2¾"h, 3½"w. **$75.00 – 100.00.**

Imperial bronze dachshund strike type table lighter, by Ronson (the tail is the striker). Circa 1940. 4"h, 9"w. **$175.00 – 250.00.**

Brass wolf table lighter (head hinged to reveal lighter). Circa 1912. 2½"h, 1½"w. **$60.00 – 100.00.**

Metal table lighters, circa 1935. (a) Elephant. 2¼"h, 2½"w. **$25.00 – 40.00.** (b) Bear. 2"h, 2½"w. **$35.00 – 50.00.**

Brass donkey, made in Japan. Circa mid 1950s. 2"h, 2½"w. **$15.00 – 20.00.**

(a) Metal tiger shaped table lighter. Circa 1935. 1¾"h, 2⅜"w. **$25.00 – 40.00.** (b) Silver-plated lion table lighter. Circa 1935. 1¾"h, 2⅜"w. **$40.00 – 70.00.**

Chromium begging dog wearing a helmet, made in Japan. Circa mid 1930s. 3⅛"h, 1¾"w. **$50.00 – 75.00.**

Brass horse head table lighter with leather reins. This lighter is lit when the reins are pulled back. Circa late 1940s. 4¾"h, 3¾"w. **$50.00 – 75.00.**

Metal camel lighter and ashtray, made in Japan. Circa early 1960s. Ashtray, 5" x 3½". Camel, 3½"h, 4"w. **$25.00 – 35.00.**

Painted metal elephant, made by Strikalite. Circa late 1940s. 3"h, 3½"w. **$30.00 – 40.00.**

Animals

Metal bull dog, made in Austria (head lifts up to reveal lighter). Dated April 2, 1912. 2¼"h, 2¾"w. **$110.00 – 140.00.**

Brass lift arm table lighter. The body of the elephant is painted metal. Circa mid 1930s. 3⅜"h, 4⅞"w. **$35.00 – 45.00.**

Bird shaped pocket lighter in brushed and smooth chromium finish. Circa 1958. 1½"h, 2⅛"w. **$20.00 – 30.00.**

Scottie dog striker table lighter, made of oxidized copper by Ronson. Circa 1936. 4"h, 5¾"w. **$250.00 – 300.00.**

Chromium houn' dog strike type table lighter, by Ronson. Circa 1934. 4½"h, 4"w. **$50.00 – 100.00.**

Chromium swan table lighter, made in Japan. Circa early 1960s. 3"h, 3¾"w. **$10.00 – 20.00.**

Dodo bird chromium strike type table lighter, by Ronson. Circa 1934. 3½"h, 4"w. **$75.00 – 110.00.**

Metal tiger table lighters, both made in Japan. Circa 1935. (a) 2⅛"h, 3"w. **$50.00 – 75.00.** (b) 2⅞"h, 2 ⅛"w. **$40.00 – 70.00.**

Painted ceramic horse table lighter, made in Japan. Circa 1955. 5½"h, 5½"w. **$15.00 – 25.00.**

Brass elephant table lighter, made in Austria. "Pat. April 2, 1912." Circa 1913. 3"h, 3½"w. **$90.00 – 115.00.**

Animals

Silver and brass lion table lighter. "Patent April 2, 1912," circa 1913. 2¾"h, 2"w. **$75.00 – 125.00.**

Metal table lighter with a poodle dog for a handle. Circa mid 1960s. 2¾"h, 2" dia. **$10.00 – 25.00.**

Gold- and silver-plated penguin table lighter. Circa 1960. 2"h, ⅞" dia. **$40.00 – 70.00.**

Ceramic duck, by Evans. Circa mid 1950s. 2¼"h, 6½"w. **$25.00 – 30.00.**

Art Deco

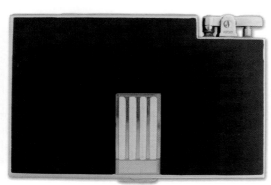

Chrome and enamel lighter/case, made by Ronson. Circa 1939. 3¼"h, 4¾"w. **$100.00 – 125.00.**

Chromium and glass airplane smoke stand. This stand contains a pipe holder, tobacco holder, and ashtray. The plane's interior and the glass base have lights for illumination during use at night. Circa mid 1930s. 37½"h, 10" dia. at base. **$400.00 – 550.00.**

Chrome and enamel lighter/case with pilot wings on front, made by Ronson. Circa 1939. 3¼"h, 4¾"w. **$100.00 – 125.00.**

The "Grecian" touch tip table lighter in chromium and tortoise enamel. Circa 1936. 3⅞"h, 2⅝" dia. at base. **$75.00 – 100.00.**

"Classic" chromium and tortoise enamel touch tip table lighter, by Ronson. Circa 1938. 3⅝"h, 3¾"w. **$150.00 – 200.00.**

Chrome and enamel lighter/case, made by Ronson. Circa 1939. 3¼"h, 4¾"w. **$100.00 – 125.00.**

Art Deco

Chrome and two-toned enamel cigarette case, made by Ronson. Circa 1930. 2½"h, 3"w. **$150.00 – 200.00.**

Chrome and enamel lighter/case, made by Ronson. Circa 1936. 2⅞"h, 4⅜"w. **$150.00 – 200.00.**

"Octette" touch tip table lighter in chromium and black enamel, by Ronson. Circa 1935. 3½"h, 3¾"w. **$100.00 – 125.00.**

Chrome and two-toned enamel lighter/case, with compact on the lid, made by Evans. Circa early 1930s. 4¼"h, 2½"w. **$100.00 – 125.00.**

Round glass ashtray and nude lady on metal base. Circa 1930. 6"h, 6¼"w. **$100.00 – 150.00.**

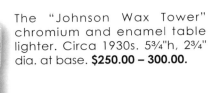

The "Johnson Wax Tower" chromium and enamel table lighter. Circa 1930s. 5¾"h, 2¾" dia. at base. **$250.00 – 300.00.**

Chrome and enamel lighter/case, made by Evans. Circa mid 1930s. 4¼"h, 2½"w. **$90.00 – 110.00.**

Bartender touch tip table lighter in chromium and walnut effect enamel, by Ronson. This lighter has cigarette compartments on each end. Circa 1936. 7"h, 6"w. **$1,400.00 – 2,000.00.**

Junior Bartender touch tip table lighter in chromium and walnut enamel, by Ronson. Circa 1937. 7½"h, 4¼"w. **$800.00 – 1,200.00.**

Bartender strike type table lighter in chromium and walnut enamel. Has a cigarette holder in the front that tips out. Made by Ronson. Circa 1936. 6⅞"h, 5⅜"w. **$1,200.00 – 1,800.00.**

Art Deco

The "Lotus" 24K gold plate and enamel table lighter, made by Ronson. Circa 1953. 2¼"h, 3¼"w. **$15.00 – 25.00.**

Chrome and tortoise enamel lighter/case with compact on the lid, made by Ronson. Circa mid 1930s. 4¼"h, 2⅝"w. **$100.00 – 125.00.**

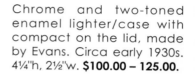

Chrome and two-toned enamel lighter/case with compact on the lid, made by Evans. Circa early 1930s. 4¼"h, 2½"w. **$100.00 – 125.00.**

Chrome and enamel lighter/case, made by Ronson. Circa 1930. 4⅛"h, 2⅝"w. **$50.00 – 75.00.**

Brass art deco lady ashtray. The base of the ashtray looks like a book. Circa 1930s. 8"h, 6"w. **$90.00 – 110.00.**

Chrome and enamel lighter/case, made by Ronson. Circa mid 1930s. 4¼"h, 2⅝"w. **$80.00 – 100.00.**

Chrome and enamel two-piece set, made by Evans. Circa late 1920s. Lighter, 2"h, 1½"w; case, 2⅞"h, 3¾"w. **$125.00 – 150.00.**

Chrome and enamel set, made by Evans. Circa 1920. Lighter, 1⅝"h, 1"w; case, 2¼"h, 3¼"w. **$150.00 – 200.00.**

The "Beautycase" in enamel and chrome finish, made by Ronson, in the box. Has a built-in lighter on the side. Circa 1936. 3"h, 4⅜"w. **$250.00 – 300.00.**

View of "Beautycase" showing the lighter.

Art Deco

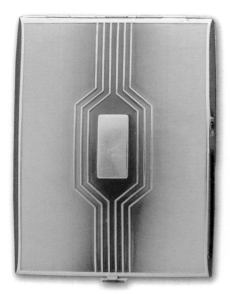

Two-piece chrome and enamel set, made by Evans. Striker lighter, 2"h, 1⅜"w; cigarette case, 2¾"h, 4"w. **$200.00 – 250.00.**

Chromium art deco design pocket lighter, made by Evans. Circa mid 1930s. 2"h, 1½"w. **$40.00 – 60.00.**

Chrome and enamel art deco style pocket lighter, made by Evans. Circa 1930s. 2"h, 1½"w. **$75.00 – 100.00.**

Ashtrays

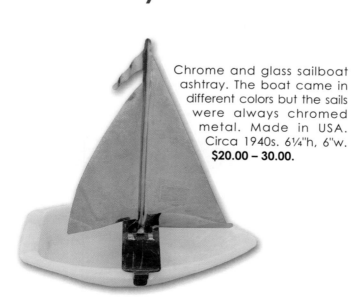

Chrome and glass sailboat ashtray. The boat came in different colors but the sails were always chromed metal. Made in USA. Circa 1940s. 6¼"h, 6"w. **$20.00 – 30.00.**

Brass lamp with an ashtray at the base (when the chain is pulled the shade lowers to reveal a cigarette holder). Circa 1950s. 8½"h, 4¼"w. **$35.00 – 50.00.**

Plastic advertising ashtray from Flanagan Funeral Home. Circa late 1900s. 1½"h, 4⅛" dia. **$10.00 – 15.00.**

Brass pocket ashtray with a lit cigarette painted on the lid. Circa early 1950s. ½"h, 3"w. **$20.00 – 30.00.**

Metal ashtray with enamel shamrock in the center, from Ireland. Circa late 1940s. ½"h, 4¾"w. **$25.00 – 35.00.**

"Cute" ceramic ashtray. Circa late 1990s. 1"h, 6⅜" dia. **$10.00 – 15.00.**

Chromium bird ashtray. Circa 1936. 2¼"h, 5¾" dia. **$20.00 – 35.00.**

Ashtrays

Ceramic ashtray, made by Adolph Coors Brewery in Golden, Colorado, for the Colorado State Fair in 1936. 1"h, 5⅞" dia. **$50.00 – 75.00.**

Metal ashtray that looks like a package of Chesterfield cigarettes (ashtray slides out). 2¼"h, 1¾"w. **$20.00 – 30.00.**

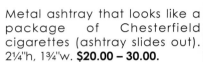

Chrome cat ashtray. Circa 1938. 2½"h, 7¼"w. **$20.00 – 40.00.**

Chrome alligator ashtray. Circa 1936. 1½"h, 4½"dia. **$20.00 – 30.00.**

Painted ceramic bellhop ashtray and cigarette holder. Circa late 1930s. 4½"h, 4"w. **$40.00 – 60.00.**

Rubber tire and glass ashtray. Circa 1930s. 1½"h, 6½"dia. **$75.00 – 100.00.**

Rubber tire with metal advertising ashtray for Firestone truck tires. Circa 1920s. 2"h, 4¼" dia. **$80.00 – 110.00.**

Closed view of a brass pocket ashtray with a painted cigarette on the lid. Circa 1950s. ½"h, 2¼"w. **$10.00 – 15.00.**

Opened view of brass pocket ashtray.

Chrome pelican ashtray. Circa 1936. 1¾"h, 4½" dia. **$20.00 – 30.00.**

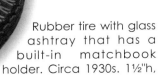

Rubber tire with glass ashtray that has a built-in matchbook holder. Circa 1930s. 1½"h, 7"dia. **$70.00 – 100.00.**

Beyond the Ordinary

Chrome and enamel lighter case and compact evening purse, made by Evans. Circa mid 1920s. Lift arm lighter, 1¾"h, 1½"w; case/compact, 2"h, 3"w. **$350.00 – 400.00.**

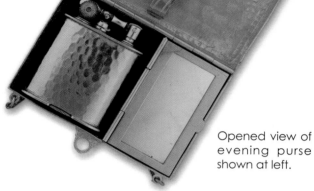

Opened view of evening purse shown at left.

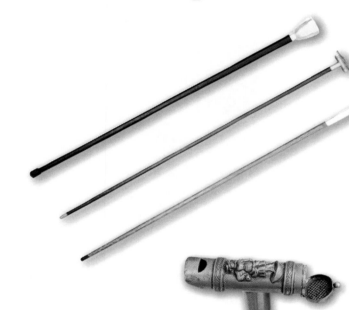

Walking canes. (a) 35¼"h, ⅞" dia. (b) 36"h, ½" dia. (c) 35"h, ⅝" dia.

Close-up of cane a with its sterling silver handle and British coin (handle unscrews to reveal the lighter), from England. Circa 1920s. Handle, 3"h, 2¼" dia. **$1,000.00 – 1,800.00.**

Close up view of cane b showing its brass-hinged match holder handle with striker on the lid. The other end has a "cat whistle" used for whistling at girls. Circa 1880s. Handle, 1⅞"h, 2½"w. **$800.00 – 1,100.00.**

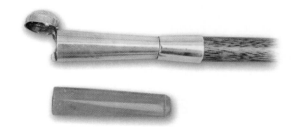

Close up view of cane c. Handle made of sterling silver, the top is hinged to reveal a cigar holder. Circa 1920s. Handle, 4"h, ⅞" dia. Cigar holder, 2⅞"h, ¾" dia. **$800.00 – 1,200.00.**

Metal box that attached to the dashboard of a car. Dispensed cigarettes, held wooden matches, and has an ashtray. Circa late 1920s. 3⅝"h, 3"w. **$125.00 – 150.00.**

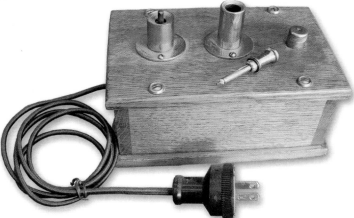

An electric cigar lighter housed in a wooden box that uses "high test" gasoline for fuel. On the left side of the top is where the gasoline was filled, the center held the wand, and on the far right is the spark housing. Made by Midwest Distributing Company in Denver, Colorado. Circa 1920s. 5⅜"h, 6½"w. **$250.00 – 300.00.**

Men's brass ring with built-in lighter. Circa late 1920s. ¾"h, ½"w. **$300.00 – 400.00.**

Beyond the Ordinary

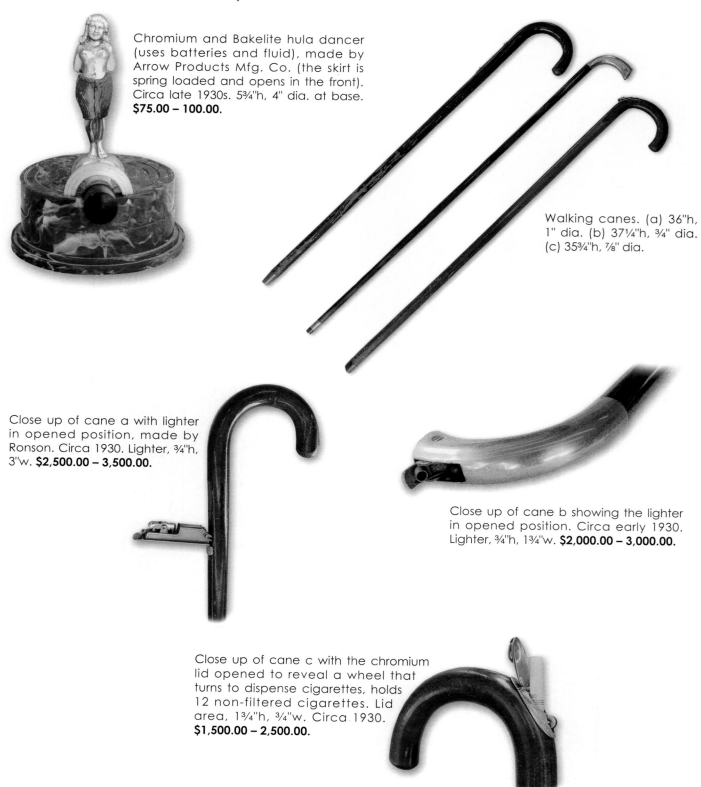

Chromium and Bakelite hula dancer (uses batteries and fluid), made by Arrow Products Mfg. Co. (the skirt is spring loaded and opens in the front). Circa late 1930s. 5¾"h, 4" dia. at base. **$75.00 – 100.00.**

Walking canes. (a) 36"h, 1" dia. (b) 37¼"h, ¾" dia. (c) 35¾"h, ⅞" dia.

Close up of cane a with lighter in opened position, made by Ronson. Circa 1930. Lighter, ¾"h, 3"w. **$2,500.00 – 3,500.00.**

Close up of cane b showing the lighter in opened position. Circa early 1930. Lighter, ¾"h, 1¾"w. **$2,000.00 – 3,000.00.**

Close up of cane c with the chromium lid opened to reveal a wheel that turns to dispense cigarettes, holds 12 non-filtered cigarettes. Lid area, 1¾"h, ¾"w. Circa 1930. **$1,500.00 – 2,500.00.**

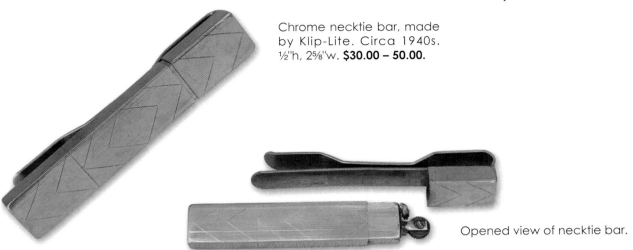

Chrome necktie bar, made by Klip-Lite. Circa 1940s. ½"h, 2⅝"w. **$30.00 – 50.00.**

Opened view of necktie bar.

Chromium and enamel table lighter, made by Silent Flame (uses fluid and batteries). Circa 1940s. 3¾"h, 2⅝" dia. at base. **$25.00 – 40.00.**

Metal striker style pocket lighter. Circa late 1930s. 2½"h, 1½"w. **$20.00 – 40.00.**

NEW METHOD SELF STARTING LIGHTER

Chromium pocket lighter with box, by New Method Mfg. Co. Circa early 1930s. 2"h, 1⅛"w. **$40.00 – 50.00.**

Beyond the Ordinary

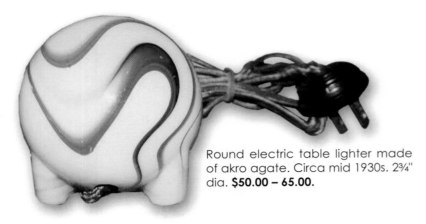

Round electric table lighter made of akro agate. Circa mid 1930s. 2¾" dia. **$50.00 – 65.00.**

Spy camera lighter with case. The camera really works with a split roll of 35mm film, made by CAMERA-LITE. Circa 1940s. 2¼"h, 1¾"w. **$300.00 – 500.00.**

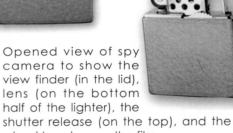

Opened view of spy camera to show the view finder (in the lid), lens (on the bottom half of the lighter), the shutter release (on the top), and the wheel to advance the film.

Electric telephone table lighter with built-in clock and ashtrays on each side. Made of metal with a painted enamel finish. Circa late 1930s. 3½"h, 11¼"w. **$75.00 – 100.00.**

Chromium pocket lighter/flashlight, operated only on batteries, made in Japan. Circa early 1960s. 2⅞"h, 1½"w. **$20.00 – 30.00.**

Chromium nude on a plastic base, used batteries and fluid, made by Dunhill. Circa 1935. 5"h, 3"w. **$70.00 – 100.00.**

Large table "Jump Spark" cigar lighter made of wood and metal. This lighter operated on batteries and fluid, and had a wick, made by Midland. Circa 1920. 15"h, 7¼"w. **$350.00 – 500.00.**

"Gloria" plastic and brass table lighter, operated on batteries and butane. Circa mid 1960s. 7¼"h, 4¼" dia. at base. **$30.00 – 50.00.**

Painted metal electric table lighter. Circa mid 1930s. 2⅛"h, 2⅜" dia. at base. **$30.00 – 45.00.**

Statue of Liberty table lighter, operates on batteries and butane. Circa mid 1950s. 7½"h, 3½"w. **$90.00 – 115.00.**

Beyond the Ordinary

"Rony" battery and butane table lighter made of plastic and metal. Circa mid 1960s. 11"h, 4⅜" dia. at base. **$40.00 – 60.00.**

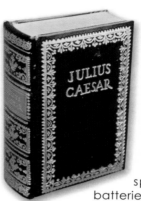

Book style table lighter. Book spine pulls open for lighting. Uses batteries and butane. Circa mid 1950s. 4"h, 2¾"w. **$40.00 – 60.00.**

Electric brass table lighter of a woman's head. The heating element is in the mouth. Circa 1920s. 7½"h, 4¼"w. **$170.00 – 230.00.**

Nude electric brass table lighter. Circa 1925. 6½"h, 3"w at base. **$90.00 – 110.00.**

"Press-A-Lite" cigarette holder and lighter made of metal and Bakelite. Has hardware to mount on a car steering column. Circa late 1940s. 2⅝"h, 3⅝"w. **$75.00 – 100.00.**

The Robot-Liter, by Ronson. Held 20 cigarettes and lit the cigarettes automatically. Made to be mounted under a car dash. Circa mid 1960s. 5¼"h, 4¼"w. **$100.00 – 150.00.**

Cheesecake

Chrome pin-up pocket lighter, made by Fire-Lite. Circa 1950s. 1⅞"h, 1⅝"w. **$25.00 – 30.00.**

Chrome pin-up pocket lighter, made by Continental. Circa 1950s. 1⅞"h, 1⅝"w. **$25.00 – 30.00.**

Chrome pin-up pocket lighter, made by Realite. Circa 1950s. 1⅞"h, 1⅝"w. **$25.00 – 30.00.**

Nude silver-plated table lighter on a marble base. Circa 1912. 7"h, 5½"w. **$150.00 – 200.00.**

Cheesecake

Chromium nude with Bakelite ashtray, made by Harry Davis Molding Co. Circa 1935. 5"h, 6¾" dia. **$40.00 – 60.00.**

Brass pocket lighter with a picture of a woman through a key hole, made by Evans. Circa 1930s. 2½"h, 1½"w. **$125.00 – 150.00.**

Chrome pocket lighter with female pin-up, made by Continental. Circa 1950. 1⅞"h, 1⅝"w. **$25.00 – 30.00.**

Brass pocket lighter with a picture of a nude woman on the front, made by Evans. Circa 1930s. 2½"h, 1½"w. **$125.00 – 150.00.**

Metal Head and Tail pocket lighter, with a key chain, by Supreme. Circa late 1950s. 1½" dia. **$25.00 – 35.00 each.**

Head and Tail lighters on a cardboard display.

"Miss Cutie" table lighter, made of gold-tone plastic with the box. Made by Negbaur. Circa mid 1950s. 4¾"h, 1½" dia. at base. **$25.00 – 50.00.**

Photos of females inside of a "Vu-Lighter" pocket lighter, made in clear plastic and chromium, by Scripto. Both circa late 1950s. 2¾"h, 1½"w. **$25.00 – 40.00 each.**

Chromium nude with a basket. Circa 1950. 6"h, ⅜" dia. at base. **$15.00 – 30.00.**

Pocket "Vu-Lighter" has metal box with instructions and guarantee, made by Scripto. Circa late 1950s. 2¾"h, 1½"w. **$40.00 – 50.00.**

Painted plastic female butane pocket lighters. Circa 1988. 3"h, 1⅛"w. **$15.00 – 20.00 each.**

Pin-up pocket lighters, in chromium, made by Supreme. Circa 1950s. 2"h, 1⅝"w. **$25.00 – 30.00 each.**

Cigarette Cases

The "Patrician" lighter/case in chrome and enamel, made by Ronson. Circa 1939. 4⅛"h, 3¼"w. **$125.00 – 150.00.**

Chrome and enamel lighter/case with compact, made by Evans. Circa early 1930s. 4¼"h, 2½"w. **$125.00 – 150.00.**

Chrome lighter/case with a unique slide mechanism on the lighter, made by Evans. Circa mid 1930s. 4¼"h, 2½"w. **$125.00 – 150.00.**

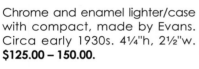

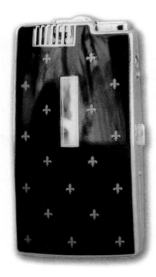

Chromium and black enamel "Mastercase" cigarette lighter/case, by Ronson. Circa 1933. 4¾"h, 2½"w. **$40.00 – 60.00.**

The "Pal" chromium and dark blue enamel, made by Ronson. Circa 1941. 4⅛"h, 2"w. **$70.00 – 100.00.**

Brass with black and white enamel cigarette lighter/case, by Marathon. Circa mid 1930s. 4¼"h, 2⅝"w. **$35.00 – 55.00.**

Chrome and brass lighter/case, made by Evans. Circa 1930s. 4⅜"h, 2⅛"w. **$75.00 – 100.00.**

Chromium and tortoise enamel "Sportcase," made by Ronson. Circa 1936. 4⅛"h, 2"w. **$60.00 – 80.00.**

Brass and enamel lighter/case with compact, made by Ronson. Circa 1933. 4¼"h, 2½"w. **$125.00 – 150.00.**

"Mastercase" chromium and tortoise enamel cigarette lighter/case, by Ronson. Circa 1933. 4⅜"h, 2½"w. **$40.00 – 60.00.**

Cigarette Cases

Gold-plate lighter/case, made by Evans. Circa mid 1930s. 4¼"h, 2½"w. **$80.00 – 100.00.**

Brass lighter/case, with oval compartment on the lid for photos, made by Marathon. Circa 1940s. 4⅛"h, 2½"w. **$60.00 – 80.00.**

Chromium "Mastercase" cigarette lighter/case, by Ronson. Circa 1933. 4⅜"h, 2⅝"w. **$25.00 – 50.00.**

Chromium and tortoise enamel lighter/case, made by Evans. Circa 1928. 4¼"h, 2⅛"w. **$115.00 – 140.00.**

Chrome and mother of pearl "Lytacase" lighter/case, made by Ronson. Circa 1929. 4¼"h, 1¾"w. **$100.00 – 125.00.**

Cigarette lighter/case, in chromium and black enamel, made by Evans. Circa late 1930s. 4¼"h, 2½"w. **$30.00 – 50.00.**

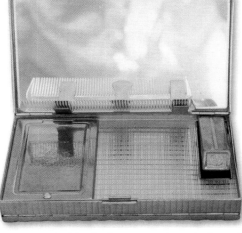

Gold-plated ladies' compact and cigarette case, made by Evans. Circa mid 1930s. 5½"h, 3⅛"w. **$125.00 – 175.00.**

Chrome and enamel lighter/case with compact in the lid, made by Evans. Circa 1930. 4¼"h, 2½"w. **$110.00 – 130.00.**

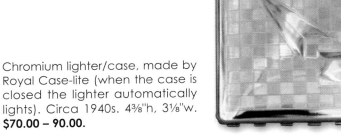

Chromium lighter/case, made by Royal Case-lite (when the case is closed the lighter automatically lights). Circa 1940s. 4⅜"h, 3⅛"w. **$70.00 – 90.00.**

Cigarette Cases

Chrome and enamel lighter/case with built-in compact, made by Evans. Circa early 1930s. 4¼"h, 2½"w. **$100.00 – 125.00.**

Chrome and enamel lighter/case, made by Evans. Circa late 1920s. 4"h, 2"w. **$125.00 – 150.00.**

Chromium cigarette case with a watch, made by Evans. Circa 1935. 4⅜"h, 3⅛"w. **$100.00 – 150.00.**

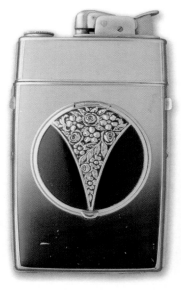

Chrome and enamel lighter/case with compact in the lid, made by Evans. Circa early 1930s. 4¼"h, 2½"w. **$100.00 – 125.00.**

Chromium and black "Twentycase" with gift box, by Ronson. Circa 1935. 4¼"h, 3"w. **$75.00 – 100.00.**

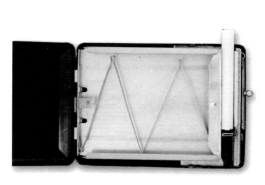
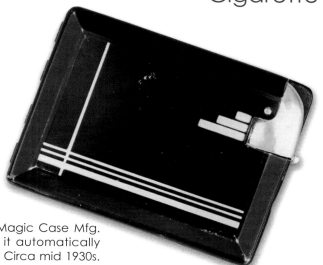

Chromium and enamel lighter/case, made by Magic Case Mfg. (when the side mechanism is pushed forward it automatically lights the cigarette and slides it out of the case). Circa mid 1930s. 4¼"h, 3⅛"w. **$75.00 – 100.00.**

Chrome and enamel lighter/case with compact in the lid, made by Marathon. Circa late 1930s. 4⅛"h, 2½"w. **$75.00 – 100.00.**

Brass and tortoise enamel cigarette lighter/case in a gift box, made by Elgin American. Circa 1940s. 3¼"h, 4⅞"w. **$70.00 – 90.00.**

Chrome and enamel lighter/case, made by Ronson. Circa 1930s. 4¼"h, 2½"w. **$25.00 – 50.00.**

Cigarette Cases

Chromium cigarette lighter/case, by Evans. Circa early 1950s. 5¾"h, 3¼"w. **$70.00 – 90.00.**

Enamel and chrome lighter/case made by Ronson. Circa 1941. 4⅛"h, 2"w. **$50.00 – 75.00.**

Chromium and black enamel cigarette lighter/case, by Evans. Circa early 1930s. 4¼"h, 2½"w. **$60.00 – 80.00.**

Chrome and enamel lighter/case, made by Evans. Circa early 1930s. 4¼"h, 2½"w. **$125.00 – 150.00.**

Chromium and black enamel cigarette lighter/case, by Evans. Circa early 1950s. 4¾"h, 2½"w. **$50.00 – 70.00.**

Ladies' brass case (with marble-like material on the lid), made by Marhill of New York. Circa early 1950s. 5¼"h, 2⅛"w. **$60.00 – 75.00.**

Chrome and enamel lighter/case with compact on the lid, made by Evans. Circa late 1920s. 4½"h, 2¼"w. **$125.00 – 150.00.**

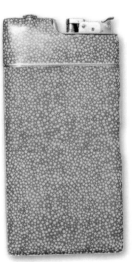

Enamel finish cigarette lighter/case, by Evans. Circa mid 1930s. 6¾"h, 3¼"w. **$60.00 – 80.00.**

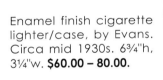

Chrome and enamel lighter/case with compact on the lid, made by Evans. Circa late 1920s. 4½"h, 2¼"w. **$125.00 – 150.00.**

Cigarette Cases

The "Pal" cigarette lighter/case, by Ronson. Circa 1941. 4⅛"h, 2"w. **$40.00 – 60.00.**

Sterling silver cigarette case. Circa mid 1930s. 3½"h, 2¼"w. **$100.00 – 125.00.**

Chrome and enamel lighter/case, made by Ronson. Circa 1935. 4¼"h, 2¼"w. **$125.00 – 150.00.**

Chromium cigarette case, by Taico. Circa 1921. 2⅞"h, 3⅞"w. **$25.00 – 40.00.**

The "Pal" chromium and tortoise enamel lighter/case, made by Ronson. Circa 1941. 4⅛"h, 2"w. **$70.00 – 90.00.**

Cigarette Cases

Brass and enamel lighter/case, with compact built into the lid, made by Newlight. Circa 1930s. 4¼"h, 2¾"w. **$75.00 – 100.00.**

Chromium cigarette case, "Pat. Mar. 2, 1926," by lymco Esector. Circa 1927. 3¾"h, 3¼"w. **$30.00 – 50.00.**

Chromium and leather "Lytacase" with a removable butane "Adonis" lighter, made by Ronson, Circa late 1950s. 5"h, 3¼"w. **$50.00 – 75.00.**

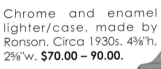

Chrome and enamel lighter/case, made by Ronson. Circa 1930s. 4⅜"h, 2⅝"w. **$70.00 – 90.00.**

Brass cigarette case with built-in watch. Circa mid 1930s. 3"h, 3¼"w. **$100.00 – 125.00.**

Cigarette Cases

Chrome and enamel lighter/case, made by Ronson. Circa 1930s. 4⅜"h, 2⅝"w. **$70.00 – 90.00.**

Cigarette lighter/case in brass and two-tone enamel. Circa early 1950s. 4½"h, 3"w. **$30.00 – 50.00.**

The "Tuxedo" in chromium and two shades of enamel, made by Ronson. Circa 1930. 4⅛"h, 2⅝"w. **$90.00 – 110.00.**

Chrome and tortoise enamel lighter/case, made by Ronson. Circa 1940. 4⅛"h, 2"w. **$40.00 – 60.00.**

Chromium lift arm cigarette lighter/case, made by Evans. Circa mid 1930s. 3⅛"h, 2½"w. **$75.00 – 90.00.**

Gold plate and tortoise enamel lighter/case, with gift box, made by Marathon. Circa mid 1930s. 4⅛"h, 2⅝"w. **$125.00 – 150.00.**

Chrome and enamel lighter/case, made by Marathon. Circa 1930s. 4⅛"h, 2½"w. **$75.00 – 100.00.**

Chromium and enamel lighter/case, made by Evans. Circa late 1930s. 4¼"h, 2½"w. **$30.00 – 50.00.**

Chrome and lighter/case, made by Ronson. Circa mid 1930s. 4"h, 3⅜"w. **$70.00 – 90.00.**

Chromium lighter/case, made for king-size cigarettes, by Evans. Circa early 1950s. 4¾"h, 2½"w. **$30.00 – 50.00.**

Cigarette Cases

Chrome and enamel lighter/case, made by Ronson. Circa mid 1930s. 4¼"h, 2⅝"w. **$75.00 – 100.00.**

Chromium and enamel lighter/case/compact, made by Evans. (Note: Due to the compact, the case only held seven cigarettes.) Circa early 1930s. 4¼"h, 2½"w. **$150.00 – 175.00.**

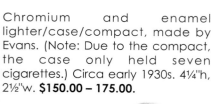

Chrome cigarette case, made by Fillkwik. Circa late 1930s. 4⅞"h, 3⅛"w. **$50.00 – 75.00.**

Chrome and enamel lighter/case, made by Ronson. Circa 1930s. 4½"h, 3⅛"w. **$50.00 – 75.00.**

Chrome and enamel lighter/case, made by Evans. Circa mid 1930s. 4¼"h, 2½"w. **$80.00 – 100.00.**

Chromium lighter/case with the U.S. Army Air Corp's emblem in blue enamel with gold trim, made by Evans. Circa early 1940s. 4¼"h, 2½"w. **$75.00 – 100.00.**

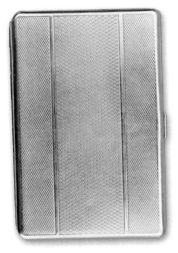

Chromium cigarette case lined in brass, made by Kincraft in England. Circa late 1940s. 5¼"h, 3⅜"w. **$45.00 – 65.00.**

Chrome and enamel lighter/case with two dogs on compact lid, made by Evans. Circa early 1930s. 4¼"h, 2½"w. **$125.00 – 150.00.**

Chromium and enamel lighter/case, made by Evans. Circa early 1930s. 4¼"h, 2½"w. **$60.00 – 80.00.**

Cigarette Cases

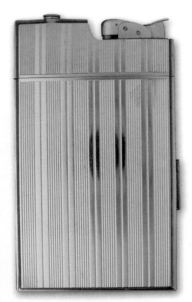

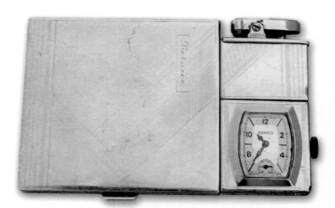

The "Kingcase" dureum finish lighter/case, made by Ronson. (Note the small second hand on the watch.) Circa 1936. 2⅞"h, 4⅜"w. **$400.00 – 500.00.**

Chrome lighter/case, made by Evans. Circa late 1930s. 5¾"h, 3¼"w. **$100.00 – 125.00.**

Brass cigarette case with the box, made by Evans. Circa mid 1930s. 3¼"h, 4⅜"w. **$80.00 – 100.00.**

Brass and enamel cigarette case, made by Evans. Circa late 1930s. 2⅛"h, 3½"w. **$80.00 – 100.00.**

Brass and mother of pearl cigarette case, made by Evans. Circa late 1930s. 3"h, 2¾"w. **$75.00 – 100.00.**

Chrome lighter/case, made by Evans. Circa late 1920s. 4⅛"h, 2⅜"w. **$125.00 – 150.00.**

Brass and jeweled lighter/case made by Evans. Circa late 1940s. Lighter, 1½"h, 1½"w. case, 2"h, 5¾"w. **$60.00 – 80.00.**

Opened view of case above.

Brass and tortoise enamel lighter/case, made by Marathon. Circa mid 1930s. 2⅞"h, 2⅞"w. **$80.00 – 100.00.**

Cigarette Cases

Three-piece chrome set with a basketweave design, made by Evans. Lighter, 2"h, 1½"w; case, 2⅞"h, 3¾"w; belt clip with chain for pocket watch, 1½"h, ⅞"w. **$200.00 – 250.00.**

Chrome and enamel two-piece set, made by Evans. Circa early 1930s. Lighter, 2"h, 1½"w; case, 3"h, 4"w. **$75.00 – 100.00.**

Chrome lighter/case, made by Evans. Circa late 1930s. 4¼"h, 2½"w. **$60.00 – 80.00.**

Chrome two-piece lighter and case, made by Bigney. Circa mid 1930s. Lighter, 2"h, 1½"w; case, 3"h, 4"w. **$175.00 – 200.00.**

Chrome and enamel lighter/case, made by Ronson. Circa 1935. 4"h, 3⅜"w. **$40.00 – 60.00.**

Chrome and enamel lighter/case, made by Ronson. Circa 1935. 4½"h, 3⅛"w. **$50.00 – 70.00.**

Metal and painted KOOL cigarette case. Circa mid 1930s. 3¼"h, 2¾"w. **$60.00 – 80.00.** (Matching lighter on page 10.)

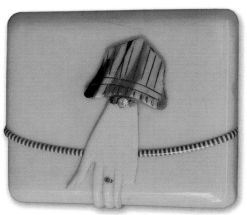

Ivory colored Bakelite cigarette case with a lady's hand holding a handbag. Circa 1930s. 3"h, 3½"w. **$30.00 – 50.00.**

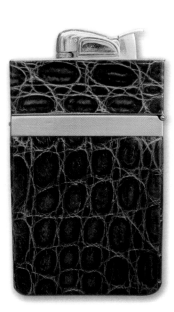

Brass and leather lighter/case, made by Evans. Circa 1930s. 4¼"h, 2⅜"w. **$50.00 – 75.00.**

Gold-tone metal cigarette case that looks like an envelope with a 3 cent postage stamp and engraving. To open push on the back side under the flap, made by Letter Case. Circa 1939. 3½"h, 5½"w. **$50.00 – 75.00.**

Cigarette Cases

Metal and tortoise enamel lighter/compact with a floral design, made by Ronson. Circa 1939. 3¼"h, 2⅞"w. **$150.00 – 200.00.**

Chrome match/cigarette case, made in USA. Small lid opens to reveal the match book then unfolds to the cigarette compartment. Circa mid 1930s. 3¾"h, 3⅛"w. **$75.00 – 100.00.**

Brass cigarette case with built-in watch, made by Watch Case Co. Circa mid 1930s. 4"h, 3"w. **$125.00 – 150.00.**

Chrome and enamel lighter/case with compact, made by Ronson. Circa 1935. 4¼"h, 2⅝"w. **$125.00 – 150.00.**

Chrome and enamel lighter/case made to hold a whole pack of cigarettes. Lighter is in the lid, made by Franklin-'54. Circa late 1940s. 3½"h, 2¼"w. **$50.00 – 75.00.**

Silver- and gold-plated match and cigarette case, made by Marathon. Circa early 1930s. Match case, 2¼"h, 1⅝"w; cigarette case, 3¾"h, 3⅛"w. **$175.00 – 200.00.**

Decorative

The "Decor" table lighter. The plastic cover can be removed to enable you to change the fabric to match your decor, made by Ronson. Circa 1954. 2¾"h, 4¼" dia. **$30.00 – 45.00.**

Brass and ceramic table lighter, made by Evans. Circa late 1930s. 6½"h, 3¼" dia. at base. **$30.00 – 50.00.**

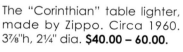

The "Corinthian" table lighter, made by Zippo. Circa 1960. 3⅞"h, 2¼" dia. **$40.00 – 60.00.**

Chromium and green and white enamel table top cigarette holder, made by Park Sherman. (To open, the top compartment rolls back.) Circa late 1930s. 2½"h, 3¾"w. **$40.00 – 60.00.**

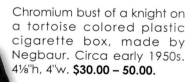

Chromium bust of a knight on a tortoise colored plastic cigarette box, made by Negbaur. Circa early 1950s. 4⅛"h, 4"w. **$30.00 – 50.00.**

Brass and marble-like plastic table lighter, made by A.S.R. Circa 1950s. 2½"h, 3"w. **$20.00 – 30.00.**

The "Cupid" table lighter, made by Ronson. This lighter has three gold cherubs on black enamel. Circa 1956. 2¼"h, 1¾" dia. **$35.00 – 50.00.**

"Nordic" table lighter in glass and chromium, made by Ronson. Circa 1955. 3½"h, 3⅜" dia. **$25.00 – 40.00.**

The "Minerva" table lighter, made by Ronson. This lighter is Ivory porcelain with a floral pattern, the lighter and base are silver plate. Circa 1952. 3 "h, 2¾"w. **$30.00 – 50.00.**

Marble base with gold-plated lighter, made by Alfred Dunhill. Circa 1955. 2½"h, 3¾"w. **$300.00 – 350.00.**

Decorative

Silver-plated "Strikalite" table lighter, made by W.B. Mfg. Co. Circa late 1940s. 4"h, 1¾" dia. at base. **$25.00 – 40.00.**

Silver-plated "Decanter" table lighter, made by Ronson. Circa 1936. 4½"h, 2½" dia. **$40.00 – 60.00.**

Marble base with brass lighter, made by Evans. Circa late 1930s. 3¾"h, 2⅛" dia. at base. **$30.00 – 35.00.**

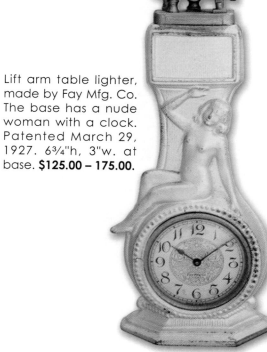

Lift arm table lighter, made by Fay Mfg. Co. The base has a nude woman with a clock. Patented March 29, 1927. 6¾"h, 3"w. at base. **$125.00 – 175.00.**

Chromium table lighter, made by A.S.R. Circa 1950s. 2½"h, 3"w. **$15.00 – 25.00.**

Silver-plated table lighter, made by Evans. Circa 1950s. 3"h, 4¼"w. **$30.00 – 45.00.**

Chromium jockey. (The back of his cap is hinged to operate lighter.) Circa early 1950s. 8½"h, 2⅞"w. at base. **$175.00 – 225.00.**

Chromium table lighter with gold trim, made by Prince. Circa mid 1950s. 2⅝"h, 2¼"w. at base. **$25.00 – 35.00.**

Gold-plated table lighter, made by Evans. Circa early 1930s. 3⅝"h, 2½"w. **$60.00 – 80.00.**

Chromium pipe table lighter with etched wooden base, made by Albert. Circa 1950s. 2⅜"h, 4½"w. **$25.00 – 40.00.**

Decorative

Crystal butane table lighter, made by Waterford in Ireland. Circa 1975. 3"h, 3½" dia. **$90.00 – 115.00.**

Chromium table lighter, made by Evans. Circa 1934. 3"h, 2¼"w. **$30.00 – 45.00.**

Bronze finished golf caddy (the bag comes off the base and the handle, where the clubs are, operates the lighter). Circa early 1930s. Caddy, 7"h, 4¼"w at base; bag, 4¾"h, 1⅜"w. **$300.00 – 350.00.**

A unique gold-plated table lighter, made by Evans. Circa 1930s. 4¾"h, 2¼"w. **$80.00 – 100.00.**

Green Wedgwood table lighter, made by Ronson. Circa 1962. 2¾"h, 2⅛"w. **$50.00 – 70.00.**

Silver-plated "Juno" table lighter, made by Ronson. Circa 1952. 6¼"h, 2" dia. at base. **$50.00 – 75.00.**

"Diana" silver-plated table lighter, made by Ronson. Circa 1950. 2¼"h, 2¾"w. **$30.00 – 40.00.**

Large chromium knight table lighter. Lights by pushing button on helmet, made by Hamilton. Circa late 1940s. 9½"h, 2⅞"w. **$60.00 – 85.00.**

Desk lighter/pen holder (when the pen holder is pushed down the lighter is lit), made in Japan. Circa 1953. 2¼"h, 3½"w. **$50.00 – 70.00.**

Chromium bust of a knight on a plastic base. The lighter is in the helmet, made by Negbaur. Circa 1950s. 3"h, 3¾"w. **$20.00 – 40.00.**

Decorative

Metal striker type knight table lighter. The striker is in the helmet and is struck on the front of the base. Circa late 1930s. 9½"h, 3⅝"w. **$80.00 – 110.00.**

Silver-plated table lighter, made in Japan. Circa late 1930s. 3¼"h, 1⅝" dia. **$30.00 – 45.00.**

Brass gold-toned apple table lighter, made by Evans. Circa mid 1950s. 3"h, 2¼" dia. **$40.00 – 60.00.**

Brass lamp post table lighter. Lights when the chain is pulled. Circa 1929. 9½"h, 3" dia. at base. **$75.00 – 100.00.**

Hand-painted egg table lighter, made by Evans. Circa mid 1950s. 2½"h, 3"w. **$60.00 – 75.00.**

Gold-plated cherubs table lighter. Circa 1935. 7"h, 3⅛" dia. at base. **$25.00 – 50.00.**

Ceramic and brass candle table lighter (spare flint in flame), made by Giv-A-Gift Inc. Circa mid 1960s. 6¼"h, 3¼" dia. **$20.00 – 40.00.**

Plastic and glass ticker tape machine table lighter, made in Japan. Circa late 1950s. 5¼"h, 3¼" dia. **$35.00 – 60.00.**

Guns

Metal spark pistol, made by Ronson. Circa 1915. 3"h, 4¾"w. **$200.00 – 300.00.**

Child's metal toy gun that shot sparks from the barrel, made by Ronson. Circa early 1930s. 4"h, 4¼"w. **$75.00 – 100.00.**

Guns

Metal and Bakelite lighter/case, made in Germany. To operate, squeeze the trigger part way and the lid to the cigarette compartment opens, pull the trigger the rest of the way and the lighter pops open and lights. Circa 1930s. 3⅛"h, 4"w. **$150.00 – 200.00.**

View of cigarettes in the handle.

Opened compartment for cigarettes and the lighter at the end of the barrel.

Small chrome pistol lighter, made in Japan. Circa late 1950s. 1½"h, 2"w. **$30.00 – 50.00.**

Pistols in chromium with black plastic grips, from Japan. Both circa mid 1950s. (a) 1½"h, 2"w. **$15.00 – 25.00.** (b) 1⅜"h, 2"w. **$15.00 – 25.00.**

Pistols. (a) All metal painted black, from Japan. Circa mid 1950s. 1½"h, 2⅛"w. **$15.00 – 25.00**. (b) Chromium with black plastic grips, from Japan. Circa mid 1950s. 1⅝"h, 2¼"w. **$15.00 – 30.00.**

Pistol spark maker used to light gas stoves, ovens etc. Has the following markings: "Shoot-A-Lite," "Safety Gas Liter," made in Germany by Larsen. "Pat. 5-16-1922," circa 1923. 3½"h, 6¼"w. **$75.00 – 100.00.**

Brass canon table lighter, made in Japan. Circa 1938. 2½"h, 5½"w. **$30.00 – 40.00.**

Brass canon table lighter, made by Negbaur. Circa 1939. 3⅛"h, 8"w. **$50.00 – 75.00.**

(a) Chromium pistol with plastic grips, made in Japan. Circa mid 1950s. 1⅜"h, 2"w. **$20.00 – 30.00**. (b) Chromium pistol with plastic grips, made in Japan. Circa mid 1950s. 1½"h, 2¼"w. **$20.00 – 30.00.**

Guns

Metal pistol (when the trigger is pulled the top half of the gun opens to light the wick), made in Austria by Dandy. Circa early 1930s. 2¼"h, 3"w. **$100.00 – 125.00.**

Brass dueling pistol table lighter, made by Dunhill. Circa 1930. 4"h, 6¼"w. **$225.00 – 300.00.**

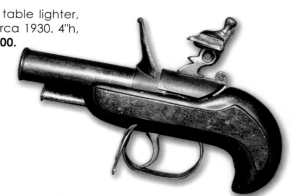

Chromium pistol with mother of pearl grips, made in Japan. Circa early 1950s. 1½"h, 2"w. **$25.00 – 40.00.**

Matches

Matchbooks from different parts of the country and businesses. Circa 1940s – present. All **$3.00 – 5.00.**

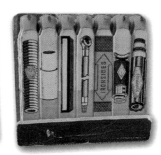

Call
1-800-833-2843
for a free
portfolio

Cremation Society
Of
New Jersey

1-800-833-2843
Thomas J. McNamara
Manager
445 Monmouth Street
Jersey City, N.J. 07306

C. Gerard Mkto, Amsterdam, NY LM

Flanagan Funeral Home, Inc.

(973) 614-1717
TERESA A. FLANAGAN,
MANAGER

583 VAN HOUTEN AVENUE
CLIFTON, NEW JERSEY 07013

C. GERARD MARKETING

Flanagan Funeral Home, Inc.

TERESA A. FLANAGAN,
MANAGER
THOMAS J. McNAMARA,
DIRECTOR

AMSTERDAM, NY-LM

Matches

Matches

Miniatures

Chromium lift arm lighter with a Japanese scene painted on, made by Perky. Circa early 1950s. ⅞"h, ¾"w. **$35.00 – 50.00.**

Chromium lift arm with mother of pearl band, with gift box, made in New York by Aladin. Circa mid 1950s. ⅞"h, ¾"w. **$40.00 – 60.00.**

Both chromium lighters, made in Japan. Circa mid 1950s. (a) 1½"h, ⅞"w. **$5.00 – 10.00.** (b) 1"h, ⅝"w. **$5.00 – 10.00.**

(a) Chromium lift arm with white leather band, made in Japan. Circa mid 1950s. ⅞"h, ¾"w. **$20.00 – 30.00.** (b) Chromium lift arm with a female on the plastic band, made in Japan. Circa mid 1950s. ⅞"h, ¾"w. **$20.00 – 35.00.**

(a) Brass pocket lighter with key chain, made by Pereline. Circa mid 1950s. 1¼"h, 1¼"w. **$5.00 – 10.00.** (b) Brass lighter with key chain, made by Royal Star. Circa mid 1950s. 1¼"h, 1¼"w. **$5.00 – 10.00.**

Chromium and painted lift arm with the state of Alaska on the front. Circa late 1950s. ⅞"h, ⅝"w. **$20.00 – 35.00.**

Chromium and leather pocket lighter, made by Continental. Circa mid 1950s. 1¼"h, 1¼"w. **$10.00 – 20.00.**

Miniatures

Small brass lighter, made in Japan. Circa 1950s. 1⅛"h, ⅝"w. **$5.00 – 10.00.**

Small brass lighter with a spring loaded wick snuffer that pivots. Circa early 1920s. 1¼"h, ⅝"w. **$125.00 – 150.00.**

Same as above showing lighter ready to light.

Small chromium lift arm lighter, made by Golden Wheel. Circa late 1940s. 1"h, ⅞"w. **$20.00 – 30.00.**

Brass lamp with enamel painted shade lighters. Circa 1950s. (a) Lighter operated by pushing the button on the base. 3½"h, 1¾" dia. at base. **$20.00 – 35.00.** (b) Pull chain under the shade to light. 4¼"h, 1⅝" dia. at base. **$15.00 – 30.00.**

Butane Coca-Cola truck, made in Japan. Lights by turning the spare tire in the back of the truck and flame comes out of the roof. Circa 1990s. 1¾"h, 3⅜"w. **$10.00 – 15.00.**

Plastic cigar lighter, made by Negbaur. Circa 1955. 2½"h, ⅝" dia. **$20.00 – 30.00.**

Butane motor cycle, made in Japan. To light, push in tail light, flame comes out of fuel tank. Circa 1990s. 2"h, 3"w. **$10.00 – 15.00.**

Novelty

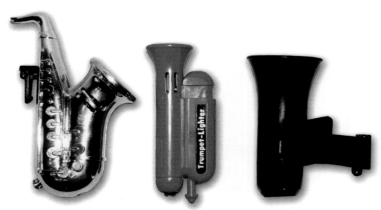

Butane chrome toilet lighter, made in Japan. Press button on bottom right side of base to light, flame comes out of bowl. Circa 1990s. 1⅞"h, 2⅜"w. **$10.00 – 15.00.**

Butane pocket lighters from Germany. All circa 1990. (a) Saxophone. 3½"h, 2"w. **$15.00 – 25.00,** (b) Trumpet. 3"h, 1¼"w. **$15.00 – 25.00,** (c) Megaphone. 2⅞"h, 2"w. **$15.00 – 25.00.**

Butane pocket lighters from Germany. All circa 1990. (a) Lowenbrau beer can. 2⅜"h, ⅞" dia. **$15.00 – 25.00.** (b) Wrench. 2⅞"h, 1¼"w. **$15.00 – 25.00.** (c) Electric drill. 2"h, 3"w. **$15.00 – 25.00.**

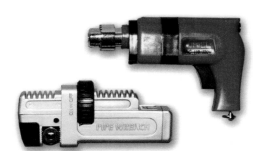

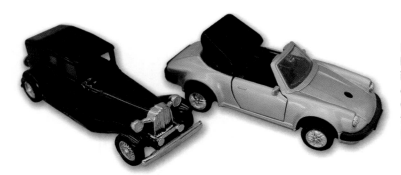

Butane sedan and convertible car lighters, made in Japan. (a) Sedan, push in on the spare tire to light, flame comes out of the hood. 1½"h, 4¼"w. (b) Convertible, push down the "boot" and flame comes out of the hood. 1½"h, 4½"w. Both circa 1990. **$10.00 – 15.00 each.**

Butane camera lighter, made in Japan. Flame comes out of top. Circa 1990s. 1¾"h, 2½"w. **$10.00 – 15.00.**

Novelty

Butane blow dryer, made in Japan. Key ring lever lights flame in the tip. Circa 1990s. 2"h, 2⅛"w. **$10.00 – 15.00.**

All butane car lighters, made in Japan. Circa 1990s. **$10.00 – 15.00 each.**

Close-up of VW bug above. Push the exhaust pipe to light. 1½"h, 2¾"w.

Close-up of MG convertible above. Push in spare tire to light, flame comes out of the hood. 1½"h, 3½"w.

Close-up of Cadillac convertible. Push the tail pipe to light. 1⅜"h, 3"w.

Novelty

Butane pocket lighters from Germany. All circa 1990. (a) Jukebox that lights up and plays music when it is lit. 2¾"h, 1⅜"w. **$15.00 – 25.00.** (b) Sun glasses. 1"h, 3½"w. **$15.00 – 25.00.** (c) Cassette tape. 1½"h, 2⅜"w. **$15.00 – 25.00.**

Twin bullet metal lighter, painted blue, made by New Method. Circa early 1930s. 2¼"h, 1⅛"w. **$20.00 – 35.00.**

Television table lighter, made by Swank. Circa early 1960s. 2¾"h, 3⅞"w. **$30.00 – 50.00.**

Butane fire extinguisher, made in Japan. Handle pulls down to light flame in nozzle. Circa 1990s. 3"h, 1¼"w. **$10.00 – 15.00.**

Butane pipe wrench, made in Japan. Top pulls back to light flame. Circa 1990s. 3⅜"h, 1"w. **$10.00 – 15.00.**

Butane Red Dog beer bottles, made in Japan. Circa 1990s. 3¼"h, ⅞"dia. **$10.00 – 15.00 each.**

Popeye the Sailor butane lighter, made in Japan. When left arm is turned the flame comes out of his pipe. Circa late 1990s. 3"h, 1¾"w. **$10.00 – 15.00.**

"Lucky Key," made of brass. Circa mid 1960s. 1¾"h, ⅜"w. **$25.00 – 40.00.**

Butane phone lighter, made in Japan. Flame comes out of dialer and rings when lit. Circa mid 1990s. 4½"h, 2½"w. **$10.00 – 15.00.**

Butane lighter in the shape of a wooden match, made in Japan. Circa late 1990s. 3½"h, ½"w. **$10.00 – 15.00.**

Novelty

Butane patriot missile, made in Japan. Flame comes out of the bottom of the missile. Circa late 1990s. 3⅞"h, 1½"w. **$10.00 – 15.00.**

Butane pocket lighters from Germany. All circa 1990. (a) Golf clubs and bag. 2⅞"h, 1⅜"w. **$15.00 – 25.00.** (b) Soccer field. 2¼"h, 1¼"w. **$15.00 – 25.00.** (c) Camera. 1½"h, 2¼"w. **$15.00 – 25.00.**

Butane pliers, hammer, and wrench, all made in Japan. Circa early 2000. Pliers, 3⅜"h, 1"w; hammer, 3½"h, 1¾"w; wrench, 3½"h, 1⅛"w. **$10.00 – 15.00 each.**

Glass of beer butane lighter, made in Japan. Flame comes out of the top of the foam. Circa 1990s. 3¼"h, 1⅛"w. **$10.00 – 15.00.**

Butane Statue of Liberty lighter, made in Japan. Pull left arm down to light the flame in the torch. Circa late 1990s. 5¼"h, 1¾"w. **$10.00 – 15.00.**

Metal yellow banana pocket lighter. Circa mid 1930s. ⅞"h, 3⅜"w. **$80.00 – 100.00**.

Model T Ford table lighter with cigarette holder, made of plastic, painted metal, and rubber. To operate lighter turn the spare tire, roll the car forward to open the cigarette holder. (Photo below shows cigarette holder and lighter lid opened.) Circa 1950. 4"h, 6½"w. **$50.00 – 70.00**.

Metal ladybug pocket lighter. Squeeze the antennas together to reveal the lighter. Circa late 1940s. ¾"h, 1¼"w. **$30.00 – 50.00**.

Novelty

Butane Budweiser beer bottle, made in China. Circa 1998. 7½"h, 2" dia. **$15.00 – 20.00.**

Pocket clip type lighters. (a) Brass and paint (looks like a pen), made by Super. Circa late 1940s. 3¼"h, ½" dia. **$15.00 – 25.00.** (b) Tin case. Circa late 1940s. 2½"h, ½"w. **$10.00 – 20.00.**

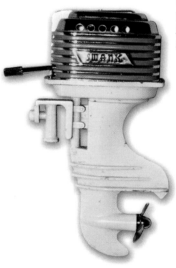

Chromium and enamel boat motor, made by SWANK. Circa early 1960s. 5"h, 2⅜"w. **$100.00 – 150.00.**

Chromium and paint table or pocket lighter with box and instructions. Circa 1940s. 3"h, ¾" dia. **$30.00 – 45.00.**

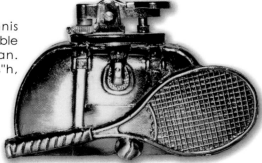

Butane chromium tennis racquet with gym bag table lighter, made in Japan. Circa early 1990s. 2⅜"h, 3⅞"w. **$15.00 – 25.00.**

Plastic butane ice skate, from Germany. Circa early 1990s. 1⅝"h, 2½"w. **$15.00 – 25.00.**

Plastic torpedo pocket lighter. Circa late 1930s. 3⅛"h, ⅝" dia. **$20.00 – 30.00.**

Plastic ice cream cone table lighter. Circa early 1960s. 3⅝"h, 2½"w. **$25.00 – 40.00.**

Metal boot lighter (lever on the back of the boot opens the lighter). Circa 1920s. 1¾"h, 2⅝"w. **$80.00 – 125.00.**

Wood and leather ski, boot, and pole table lighter. Circa mid 1960s. 2¾"h, 9⅛"w. **$15.00 – 25.00.**

Novelty

Chromium bottles with paper labels table or pocket lighters, made by KEM Inc., Lightrs. Circa 1948. 2⅝"h, ⅝" dia. **$20.00 – 30.00 each.**

Brass Model T Ford (to operate the lighter press the horn on the left side of the hood), made in Japan. Circa mid 1950s. 3⅛"h, 5"w. **$20.00 – 35.00.**

Brass locomotive table lighter (roof hinged to reveal the lighter). Circa early 1960s. 2¼"h, 4¾"w. **$20.00 – 40.00.**

Brass tank table lighter that lights by pushing the button on the rear of the tank. Circa early 1950s. 1¾"h, 5¾"w. **$30.00 – 65.00.**

Small Sarome "Blue Bird" table or pocket lighter. Made of painted chromium. Circa mid 1960s. 1⅛"h, 3⅛"w. **$25.00 – 45.00.**

Ceramic beer stein table lighter, from Germany. Circa 1958. 3¾"h, 1⅝" dia. **$45.00 – 60.00.**

Wooden barrel table lighter with a painted swan. Circa 1960s. 3¾"h, 2" dia. **$15.00 – 25.00.**

Brass stove (chimney comes off to reveal lighter). Circa mid 1950s. 3¼"h, ½"w. **$10.00 – 20.00.**

Brass golf clubs and bag, made by Negbaur. Circa 1939. 5"h, 1½"w. **$75.00 – 100.00.**

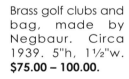

Cowboy boot table lighter, made by Evans. Circa 1948. 5"h, 5"w. **$40.00 – 60.00.**

Novelty

Barrette, made by Stuart (perfume bottles converted to lighters). Circa 1939. 4¾"h, 5"w. **$45.00 – 60.00.**

Slot machine table lighter that operates on batteries and butane (when the arm is pulled the window view spins around and the flame lights from above). Circa mid 1960s. 6¾"h, 6"w. **$30.00 – 45.00.**

Chromium and plastic touch tip style engine table lighter, made by Remler Co. Ltd. Circa 1947. 3½"h, 5¼"w. **$125.00 – 175.00.**

Wooden shoe with painting on top done by hand, this is a souvenir of Holland. Circa 1940s. 2⅛"h, 4½"w. **$20.00 – 40.00.**

Occupied Japan

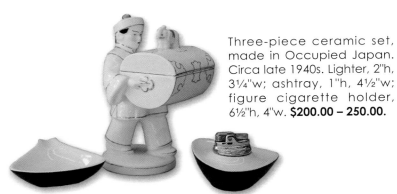

Three-piece ceramic set, made in Occupied Japan. Circa late 1940s. Lighter, 2"h, 3¼"w; ashtray, 1"h, 4½"w; figure cigarette holder, 6½"h, 4"w. **$200.00 – 250.00.**

Chromium bird cage table lighter (the bird feeder at the bottom of the cage is the lighter), made in Occupied Japan. Circa early 1950s. 5½"h, 4"w. **$200.00 – 250.00.**

Chrome table lighter, made in Occupied Japan. When wand is pulled out, the lighter's mechanism strikes the flint. Circa late 1940s. 4¼"h, 2⅝" dia. **$150.00 – 200.00.**

Chromium car table lighter (when the button on the left fender is pushed the hood opens and the lighter is lit), made in Occupied Japan. Circa 1948. 1"h, 3"w. **$80.00 – 110.00.**

Chrome table lighter set, made in Occupied Japan. Circa early 1950s. Lighter, 3⅛"h, 2¼"w; cigarette holder, 3⅛"h, 2½"w; ashtrays, 3" dia.; tray, 4½"h, 9½"w. **$200.00 – 250.00.**

Occupied Japan

Chromium rocket ship table lighter (squeeze the rear fins together to light), made in Occupied Japan. Circa 1949. 2"h, 5⅛"w. **$80.00 – 110.00.**

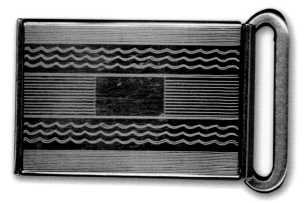

Chrome belt buckle, made in Occupied Japan. Circa late 1940s. 1¼"h, 1⅞"w. **$150.00 – 200.00.**

Chromium lift arm pocket lighter with mother of pearl inlay, made in Occupied Japan. Circa 1948. Front and back views shown. 2⅛"h, 1½"w. **$80.00 – 110.00.**

Chrome lighter/case, made in Occupied Japan. Circa Late 1940s. 4⅜"h, 2⅜"w. **$150.00 – 200.00.**

Chromium camera with leather band, a tripod with telescoping legs, and a gift box, made in Occupied Japan. Circa 1948. 3⅞"h. 2⅝"w. **$100.00 – 125.00.**

Chrome and enamel lighter/case, made in Occupied Japan. Circa late 1940s. 4"h, 2½"w. **$200.00 – 250.00.**

Miniature chromium lift arm pocket lighter, made in Occupied Japan. Circa 1948. 1"h, ⅞"w. **$30.00 – 50.00.**

Chrome and enamel lighter/case, made in Occupied Japan. Circa late 1940s. 3¾"h, 2¼"w. **$150.00 – 200.00.**

Occupied Japan

Silver-plated three-piece set, made in Occupied Japan. Circa 1948. Lighter, 3"h, 2¾" dia.; cigarette holder, 2¾"h, 2¾" dia.; tray, 4" x 7¼". **$80.00 – 100.00.**

Metal and Bakelite radio table lighter, made in Occupied Japan. Circa late 1940s. 2⅝"h, 2"w. **$150.00 – 200.00.**

Two-piece chromium set, made in Occupied Japan. Circa 1949. Lighter, 3"h, 4"w; ashtray, 3¼" x 5½". **$75.00 – 90.00.**

Chrome horse shoe lighter with a horse head, made in Occupied Japan. Circa 1940s. 3"h, 2¼"w. **$125.00 – 150.00.**

Large chromium lift arm table lighter, made in Occupied Japan. Circa 1950. 3⅞"h, 2⅞"w. **$100.00 – 125.00.**

Chrome football, made in Occupied Japan. Circa late 1940s. 2¾"h, 2¾"w. **$125.00 – 175.00.**

Chromium lift arm table lighter with mother of pearl inlays, made in Occupied Japan. Circa 1948. 2⅛"h, 2"w at base. **$80.00 – 100.00.**

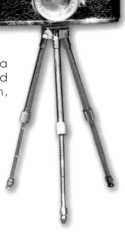

Camera table lighter on a tripod, made in Occupied Japan. Circa 1948. 5"h, 2¾"w. **$90.00 – 110.00.**

Brass finished fish table lighter, made in Occupied Japan. Circa late 1940s. 3"h, 3¼"w. **$125.00 – 150.00.**

Chrome lizard covered lift arm pocket lighter, made in Occupied Japan. Circa late 1940s. 1½"h, 1"w. **$50.00 – 75.00.**

Occupied Japan

Ceramic and metal lamp with pink flamingo table lighter, made in Occupied Japan. Lighter is in the top of the lamp shade. Circa 1940s. 5¼"h, 3½"w. **$90.00 – 110.00.**

Metal, chromium, and leather camera on a tripod with a shutter release cable to operate lighter, made in Occupied Japan. Circa 1948. 3"h, 2½"w. **$80.00 – 100.00.**

Chrome horse head lighter, made in Occupied Japan. Circa 1940s. 3⅛"h, 3"w. **$75.00 – 100.00.**

Chromium lift arm lighters with leather bands and attached key chain, made in Occupied Japan. Circa 1948. (a) ⅞"h, ¾"w. (b) ⅞"h, ⅞"w. **$20.00 – 40.00 each.**

Chrome and enamel lighter/case (showing striker removed), made in Occupied Japan. Striker lights at the top of the case. Circa late 1940s. 3¾"h, 2½"w. **$150.00 – 200.00.**

Chromium lift arm lighters, made in Occupied Japan. Circa 1948. (a) Has a unique flint wheel, 7/8"h, 7/8"w. **$40.00 – 60.00.** (b) 7/8"h, 7/8"w. **$20.00 – 40.00.**

Both chromium lift arm table lighters with mother of pearl on the front and back, made in Occupied Japan. Circa 1948. 1¼"h, 1⅜"w at base. **$35.00 – 45.00 each.**

Chrome coffee pot lighter, made in Occupied Japan. Circa late 1940s. 3"h, 3¼"w. **$75.00 – 100.00.**

Chromium lift arm with metal band, made in Occupied Japan. Circa 1948. 1⅝"h, 1⅛"w. **$30.00 – 50.00.**

Chrome lighter in ceramic base, made in Occupied Japan. Circa late 1940s. 3"h, 2½" dia. **$75.00 – 100.00.**

Occupied Japan

Chromium lift arm lighters with leather bands both, made in Occupied Japan. Circa 1948. (a) 1"h, 1"w. (b) 1⅛"h, ⅞"w. **$30.00 – 45.00 each.**

Chrome table lighter, made in Occupied Japan. Circa 1940s. 2½"h, 2¼"w. **$75.00 – 100.00.**

Chrome table lighter, made in Occupied Japan. Circa late 1940s. 2⅞"h, 2"w. **$80.00 – 100.00.**

Chromium pocket lighter, made in Occupied Japan. Circa 1940s. 1⅞"h, 1¾"w. **$125.00 – 150.00.**

Chromium and mother of pearl pistol lighter, made in Occupied Japan. Circa late 1940s. 2¼"h, 3"w. **$60.00 – 80.00.**

Chromium and mother of pearl pistol lighter, made in Occupied Japan. Circa late 1940s. 2"h, 2¾"w. **$65.00 – 85.00.**

Chromium with mother of pearl grips pistol lighter, made in Occupied Japan. Circa late 1940s. 2¼"h, 3"w. **$60.00 – 80.00.**

Chrome lighter, made in Occupied Japan. Has plastic inserts in the grip and a unique lighter cover on the top right side of the gun. Circa late 1940s. 1⅞"h, 2⅝"w. **$100.00 – 150.00.**

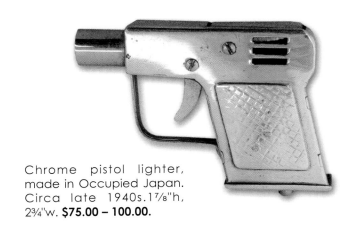

Chrome pistol lighter, made in Occupied Japan. Circa late 1940s. 1⅞"h, 2¾"w. **$75.00 – 100.00.**

Silver-plated table lighter, made in Occupied Japan. Circa 1948. 2¼"h, 2½"w. **$60.00 – 80.00.**

Occupied Japan

Unusual chrome pistol lighter, made in Occupied Japan. Circa 1940s. 1½"h, 2⅞"w. **$150.00 – 200.00.**

Brass dog with front paws on a fence looking at a book (the book is the lighter), made in Occupied Japan. Circa 1948. 2⅝"h, 2⅜"w. **$80.00 – 120.00.**

Chromium pistol table lighter on a stand, made in Occupied Japan. Circa 1949. 2½"h, 3½"w. **$75.00 – 100.00.**

Chromium pistol with black plastic grips on a stand, made in Occupied Japan. Circa 1949. 2½"h, 3¾"w. **$70.00 – 90.00.**

(a) Chromium pistol with plastic grips, made in Occupied Japan. Circa 1949. 2"h, 2¾"w. **$30.00 – 60.00.** (b) Chromium pistol with plastic grips, made in Occupied Japan. Circa early 1950s. 2¼"h, 3"w. **$50.00 – 70.00.**

Chromium pistol with plastic grips on a stand, made in Occupied Japan. Circa 1949. 2½"h, 3½"w. **$70.00 – 90.00.**

Chromium pistols with mother of pearl handles, both made in Occupied Japan. Both circa 1949. (a) 1⅛"h, 1½"w. **$40.00 – 60.00.** (b) 2"h, 3"w. **$70.00 – 90.00.**

Both chromium pistols, made in Occupied Japan. Circa 1949. (a) Has plastic grips. 2¾"h, 3¾"w. **$60.00 – 80.00.** (b) Has mother of pearl grips. 3"h, 3⅞"w. **$70.00 – 90.00.**

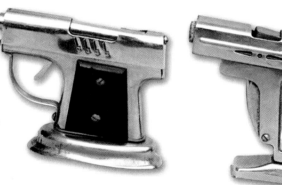

"Patricia" silver-plated over blue glass table lighter, made in Occupied Japan. Circa 1949. 3¼"h, 4½"w. **$90.00 – 110.00.**

Silver-plated table lighter, made in Occupied Japan. Circa 1948. 2¾"h, 3"w. **$50.00 – 70.00.**

Occupied Japan

Chromium ship table lighter with red plastic along the bottom of the lighter, made in Occupied Japan. Circa 1950. 2"h, 5"w. **$75.00 – 90.00.**

Silver cowboy boot table lighters, made in Occupied Japan. Circa 1950. (a) Has roses on boot. 3"h, 3½"w. **$50.00 – 70.00.** (b) Has flowers on the side of the boot and stitching on the toe. 2¾"h, 2¾"w. **$50.00 – 70.00.**

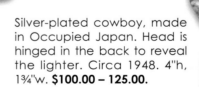

Silver-plated cowboy, made in Occupied Japan. Head is hinged in the back to reveal the lighter. Circa 1948. 4"h, 1¾"w. **$100.00 – 125.00.**

Silver-plated cowboy boot table lighters. (a) Has a cowboy riding a horse on the side (this boot was made without a spur), made in Occupied Japan. Circa 1950. 3¼"h, 3¼"w. **$65.00 – 80.00.** (b) Tall boot with a flowery vine on the side, made in Occupied Japan. Circa 1950. 4¼"h, 3½"w. **$50.00 – 75.00.**

Chromium and plastic microphone, made in Occupied Japan. Circa late 1940s. 4⅞"h, 1⅞"w. **$175.00 – 200.00.**

Silver-plated emperor table lighter, made in Occupied Japan. Circa 1948. 3¼"h, 3½"w. **$50.00 – 70.00.**

Chromium and mother of pearl lift arm pocket lighter, made in Occupied Japan. Circa 1948. 1⅞"h, 1⅝"w. **$115.00 – 140.00.**

Chromium and ceramic elephant table lighter, made in Occupied Japan. Circa 1948. 3½"h, 4"w. **$90.00 – 125.00.**

Chromium and plastic piano table lighter (push down on the keyboard to light), made in Occupied Japan. Circa 1948. 3¼"h, 2⅝"w. **$115.00 – 130.00.**

Occupied Japan

Silver-plated barrel table lighter, made in Occupied Japan. Circa 1948. 3"h, 1¾" dia. **$60.00 – 80.00.**

Silver-plated cowboy boot with sunburst on the front and floral design on the back, made in Occupied Japan (this boot was made without a spur). Circa 1950. 2⅞"h, 2⅞"w. **$60.00 – 80.00.**

Silver-plated owl table lighter with glass eyes, made in Occupied Japan. Circa 1948. 3' h, 2'w. **$90.00 – 110.00.**

Chromium telephone table lighter (take the receiver off and turn the dial to operate lighter), made in Occupied Japan. Circa 1948. 2¼"h, 3½"w. **$100.00 – 130.00.**

Chromium typewriter, made in Occupied Japan (lights by pressing space bar). Circa 1948. 1¾"h, 3½"w. **$175.00 – 200.00.**

Silver-plated bellhop with suitcase, made in Occupied Japan (to light, pick up the lighter and it automatically lights, the flame comes out of the top of suitcase). Circa 1948. 4½"h, 3½"w. **$200.00 – 250.00.**

Silver-plated lighthouse table lighter, made in Occupied Japan. Circa 1948. 4¼"h, 1½" dia. at base. **$60.00 – 90.00.**

Sewing machine with plastic cigarette holder in the base, made in Occupied Japan (lights by the needle). 3"h, 4"w. **$175.00 – 200.00.**

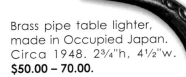

Brass pipe table lighter, made in Occupied Japan. Circa 1948. 2¾"h, 4½"w. **$50.00 – 70.00.**

Silver-plated barrel table lighter, made in Occupied Japan. Circa 1948. 3⅛"h, 1¾"dia. **$70.00 – 100.00.**

Occupied Japan

Metal gas pump table lighter (squeeze the nozzle to operate lighter), made in Occupied Japan. Circa 1949. 3½"h, 1¼"w. **$75.00 – 100.00.**

Ceramic cat with lamp on a book and hand-painted lamp shade (pull chain under the shade to light), made in Occupied Japan. Circa 1948. 5¼"h, 2¾"w. **$90.00 – 110.00.**

Knight table lighters, all made in Occupied Japan. All circa 1948. (a) 3½"h, 1½"w. (b) Made without a shield but has a stand. 4"h, 1½"w. (c) 3½"h, 1½"w. **$75.00 – 90.00 each.**

All chromium with mesh bands, made in Occupied Japan. Circa 1949. (a) 1½"h, 1⅛"w. **$30.00 – 50.00.** (b) 1⅛"h, ⅞"w. **$30.00 – 50.00.** (c) ⅞"h, ¾"w. **$35.00 – 50.00.** (d) ¾"h, ¾"w. **$35.00 – 50.00.**

Pocket Lighters

Brass and enamel compact shaped lighter, made by Plaza Lighter Co. Lights when opened. ½"h, 2¼" dia. **$60.00 – 80.00.**

Front and back views of brass pocket lighters (the wick cap has to be unscrewed and taken off to light). Circa 1918. (a) 3⅛"h, 2⅜"w. **$100.00 – 150.00.** (b) 3"h, 2⅜"w. **$100.00 – 150.00.**

Unique pocket lighter with duel wicks. One on a pull chain and one under a screw cap. (Supposedly the city of St. Louis gave the lighters to all the soldiers in the 35th Division who fought in France). Circa 1918. 3¼"h, 2"w. **$275.00 – 375.00.**

Pocket Lighters

Chrome with delft ceramic inlay, made by Evans. Circa mid 1930s. 2"h, 1½"w. **$50.00 – 70.00.**

The "Trickette" brass and rhinestone pocket lighter, made by Wisner. Circa early 1950s. 1½"h, 1¾"w. **$25.00 – 40.00.**

Brass pocket lighters shaped like books. Both circa 1918. Both 2½"h, 1¾"w. **$100.00 – 150.00 each.**

Chromium pocket lighter with a unique floral design, made by Evans. Circa late 1940s. 2"h, 1½"w. **$35.00 – 50.00.**

Chrome pocket lighter with pilot wings, made by Evans. Circa late 1930s. 2"h, 1½"w. **$50.00 – 75.00.**

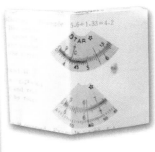

The "Renown" pocket lighter, made by Corona. This lighter has a built in slide rule on the front. Shown with the instructions and gift box. Circa 1945. 2¼"h, 1½"w. **$100.00 – 125.00.**

Brass pocket lighter, by Snap-A-Lite. Circa 1913. 2½"h, 1"w. **$40.00 – 60.00.**

Brass violin striker lighter. Circa 1920s. 2½"h, ¾"w. **$200.00 – 300.00.**

Violin shown with striker removed.

Chromium lift arm pocket lighter, made by Colibri. Circa 1928. 2"h, 1⅝"w. **$200.00 – 250.00.**

Pocket Lighters

Chromium pocket lighter (remove the cap to operate lighter). Circa 1922. 2⅛"h, 1¼"w. **$30.00 – 50.00.**

Gold- and brass-tone lighter, made by Evans. Circa late 1930s. 2"h, 1½"w. **$75.00 – 100.00.**

Round brass pocket lighters. Both circa 1918. Shown are front and back views of each. (a) Has unique slide cap over the wick. 2½"h, 1¾"w. **$125.00 – 150.00.** (b) 2½"h, 1¾"w. **$125.00 – 150.00.**

Brass butane lighter in gift box, made by Scripto. Circa late 1950s. 2½"h, 1¼"w. **$30.00 – 50.00.**

Gold-tone Mr. & Mrs. lighter set, made by Evans. Circa late 1940s. Mr., 2½"h, 1½"w; Mrs., 1½"h, 1½"w. **$125.00 – 150.00.**

Chromium butane pocket lighter, made by Colibri in Ireland. Circa early 1960s. 3"h, ⅞"w. **$60.00 – 85.00.**

Chromium pocket lighter, made in Austria. Circa 1925. 2½"h, 1¼"w. **$35.00 – 55.00.**

Ladies' brass and leather covered pocket lighter, made in Germany. Circa mid 1950s. 1⅜"h, 1½"w. **$40.00 – 50.00.**

Leather flap opened to view lighter.

Pocket Lighters

Chrome His & Hers lighter set, made by Stebco. Circa 1950s. His, 1⅞"h, 2"w; Hers, 1½"h, 1⅝"w. **$40.00 – 60.00.**

Chromium pocket lighter, by Novitas Sales Co. Circa 1920. 2⅝"h, 1"w. **$50.00 – 70.00.**

Brass with plaid band pocket lighter made by Evans. Circa late 1930s. 1½"h, 1½"w. **$25.00 – 30.00.**

Black plastic and chromium pocket lighter, made by LECTRoLITE. Circa 1930s. 2"h, 1½"w. **$30.00 – 40.00.**

Platinum plate pocket lighter, made by LECTRoLITE. Circa late 1930s. 1¾"h, 1⅝"w. **$40.00 – 50.00.**

Chrome pocket lighter with a funny decal on the front, made by Evans. Circa late 1930s. 2 "h, 1½"w. **$35.00 – 45.00.**

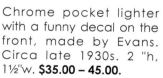

Gold-tone musical pocket lighter, made by Crown. Circa late 1940s. 2⅝"h, 1⅜"w. **$30.00 – 50.00.**

Chromium with leather band lift arm pocket lighter, made by Superfine. Circa late 1920s. 1⅞"h, 1½"w. **$70.00 – 90.00.**

Brass with leather band pocket lighter, made by Evans. Circa late 1940s. 2½"h, 1½"w. **$25.00 – 40.00.**

Brass and chromium pocket lighter, made by Evans. Circa 1930s. 2"h, 1½"w. **$35.00 – 50.00.**

Brass and enamel pocket lighter with a unique windscreen (it was sometimes used as a table lighter because of its size and beauty), made by Evans. Circa 1934. 2⅜"h, 2¼"w. **$40.00 – 50.00.**

Pocket Lighters

Brass with ceramic inlay with flower design pocket lighter, made by Evans. 2"h, 1½"w. **$30.00 – 45.00.**

Brass pocket lighter with unique slide cap over the wick, made by Parker in Austria. "U.S. Pat. Apr. 2, 1912." Circa 1913. 2⅜"h, 1¼"w. **$70.00 – 90.00.**

Chrome pocket lighter, made by Evans. Circa late 1920s. 2"h, 1½"w. **$60.00 – 75.00.**

The Zippo fifth year anniversary pocket ighter (1932 – 1937) with the Zippo Lady etched on chromium, made by Zippo. Circa 1993. 2¼"h, 1½"w. **$30.00 – 40.00.**

Brass and Bakelite lift arm pocket lighter, made by MAY FAIR. Circa mid 1930s. 2"h, 1⅝"w. **$70.00 – 90.00.**

Battle ship U.S.S *Hayler* DD 997 chromium pocket lighter, made by Zippo. Circa 1994. 2¼"h, 1½"w. **$30.00 – 40.00 each.**

Sterling silver lift arm pocket lighter, made in Mexico. Circa late 1930s. 1⅝"h, 1⅝"w. **$30.00 – 55.00.**

Chrome pocket lighter with a unique slide mechanism, made by Evans. Circa 1930s. 2"h, 1½"w. **$75.00 – 100.00.**

Chromium pocket lighter, made by Perfecto. Circa 1930. 2½"h, 1½"w. **$40.00 – 55.00.**

"Oliver" pocket lighter (can also be used as a small table lighter by pivoting the outside frame) in chrome finish, made by Cherrylite. Circa mid 1950s. 1⅝"h, 2⅜"w. **$50.00 – 70.00.**

Pocket Lighters

Chromium pocket lighter, made by Thorens. Circa early 1930s. 2⅜"h, 1½"w. **$50.00 – 65.00.**

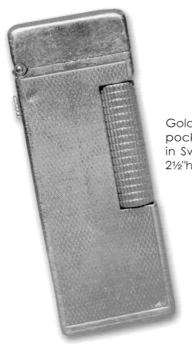

Gold-plated butane lift arm style pocket lighter, made by Dunhill in Switzerland. Circa mid 1950s. 2½"h, ⅞"w. **$250.00 – 325.00.**

Chromium lift arm pocket lighter, made by TEE-VEE. Circa mid 1930s. 2¼"h, 1"w. **$15.00 – 25.00.**

Chrome and enamel pocket lighter with gold-tone pilot wings on the front, made by Evans. Circa late 1930s. 2"h, 1½"w. **$45.00 – 60.00.**

Chromium lighter that has a unique thumb slide action lever on the side to operate, made by Thorens in Switzerland. Circa late 1940s. 2⅝"h, 1"w. **$75.00 – 100.00.**

Brass submarine pocket lighter. Circa 1918. 1½"h, 3¼"w. **$100.00 – 150.00.**

Open view of submarine lighter.

Silver-plated lift arm pocket lighter, made by Evans. Circa late 1920s. 1⅞"h, 1½"w. **$90.00 – 115.00.**

Chromium pocket lighter with lift off wick cap, made by Derby. "Patented April 2, 1912." Circa 1913. 2½"h, ⅞"w. **$50.00 – 70.00.**

The "Princess" chromium pocket lighter with a leather band, made by Ronson. Circa 1950s. 1⅞"h, 1½"w. Circa 1950s. **$45.00 – 60.00.**

Pocket Lighters

Chromium shoe pocket lighter, made in Austria. Circa 1912. 1½"h, 2"w. **$150.00 – 200.00.**

Opened view of shoe lighter.

Chromium pocket lighter, made by Thorens (Swiss made). Circa early 1920s. 2¼"h, 1⅝"w. **$60.00 – 75.00.**

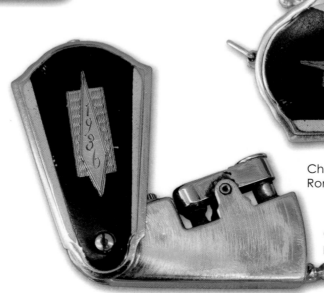

Chrome and enamel "Vee" pocket lighter, made by Ronson. Circa 1936. 2¼"h, 1¼"w. **$250.00 – 300.00.**

Opened view of "Vee" pocket lighter.

Chromium butane pocket lighter, made by Bentley in Austria. Circa late 1950s. 2¼"h, 1½"w. **$20.00 – 40.00.**

Round brass pocket lighters. (Front and back designs shown.) Both circa 1918. (a) Wick cap unscrews. 2⅜"h, 1⅝"w. **$125.00 – 150.00.** (b) Has a unique lift arm. 2¼"h, 1⅝"w. **$175.00 – 200.00.**

Chromium and enamel lighter, made by Imaco. Circa late 1950s. 2¼"h, 1½"w. **$20.00 – 30.00.**

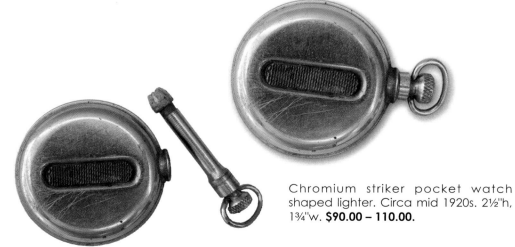

Chromium striker pocket watch shaped lighter. Circa mid 1920s. 2½"h, 1¾"w. **$90.00 – 110.00.**

View of pocket watch lighter with striker removed.

Pocket Lighters

Chromium lift arm pocket lighter, made by Paramount. Circa mid 1920s. 1¾"h, 1½"w. **$80.00 – 90.00.**

Chromium lift arm pocket lighter that has a unique built-in windscreen, made by Polo in England. Circa mid 1930s. 2"h, 1⅝"w. **$100.00 – 120.00.**

Chromium pocket watch style lighter, made by Chronos (push in top of knob to light). Circa 1930s. 2⅝"h, 1⅞"w. **$100.00 – 120.00.**

Chromium pocket with a built-in windshield. Circa 1932. 2⅛"h, 1½"w. **$40.00 – 60.00**

Chrome pocket lighter, made by Evans, with a comic drawing on the front. Circa late 1930s. 2"h, 1¼"w. **$45.00 – 60.00.**

Chromium foxhole style pocket lighter. Circa early 1940s. 2½"h, ⅞"w. **$30.00 – 40.00.**

Two-tone brass and gold lighter made by Evans. Circa 1930s. 2"h, 1¾"w. **$75.00 – 100.00.**

Silverplate with a unique slide bar on the top left side to open lighter. Circa mid 1930s. 1¾"h, 2"w. **$100.00 – 125.00.**

Chromium butane pipe lighter, made by Savinelli. Circa mid 1970s. 2¾"h, 1⅛"w. **$25.00 – 40.00.**

Brass pocket lighters (front and back designs shown). Both circa 1918. (a) 2½"h, 1¾"w. **$100.00 – 150.00.** (b) 2⅜"h, 1¾"w. **$125.00 – 150.00.**

Pocket Lighters

Gold-tone pocket lighter with a watch, made by Rivo. Circa early 1950s. 2⅛"h, 1"w. **$80.00 – 100.00.**

Reproduction of Ronson's "Banjo" lighter in gold plate and enamel finish. Circa 1960s. 2⅜"h, 1⅞"w. **$60.00 – 80.00.**

Chromium lift arm style pocket lighter, by TEE-VEE. Circa mid 1930s. 1½"h, ⅞"w. **$15.00 – 25.00.**

Chromium finish pocket lighter, made by Evans. Circa late 1940s. 2"h, 1½"w. **$40.00 – 60.00.**

Chrome lighter with a watch in a gift box, from Macy's Men's Store in New York, made by Swank. Circa early 1950s. 2⅜"h, 1⅛"w. **$100.00 – 125.00.**

Brass with a leather band, made by Evans. Circa late 1940s. 2½"h, 1½"w. **$25.00 – 40.00.**

Brass pocket lighter in a gift box, made by Evans. Circa late 1930s. 2"h, 1⅞"w. **$45.00 – 65.00.**

Brass pocket lighter, made in Austria. Circa 1925. 2⅜"h, 1½"w. **$35.00 – 50.00.**

Chrome and enamel pocket lighter with a watch, made by Windsor. Circa early 1950s. 2¼"h, 1⅝"w. **$75.00 – 100.00.**

Chromium foxhole style lighter. Circa early 1940s. 1⅞"h, ¾"w. **$30.00 – 40.00.**

Pocket Lighters

Silver lift arm pocket lighter, made by Colibri. Circa 1937. 2½"h, 1⅜"w. **$110.00 – 140.00.**

Silver-plated pocket lighter, made by Evans. Circa early 1930s. 2½"h, ¾"w. **$150.00 – 200.00.**

Unique chrome and enamel pocket lighter, made in Austria. Circa mid 1930s. 2⅛"h, 1⅛"w. **$125.00 – 150.00.**

Chrome "De-Light" pocket lighter, made by Ronson. Circa 1928. 2⅝"h, 1½"w. **$50.00 – 75.00.**

The Zippo American Eagle in chromium finish (each lighter has been individually numbered). Circa 1994. 2¼"h, 1½"w. **$40.00 – 60.00.**

"Standard" chromium pocket lighter, by Ronson. Circa 1935. 2"h, 1⅝"w. **$50.00 – 70.00.**

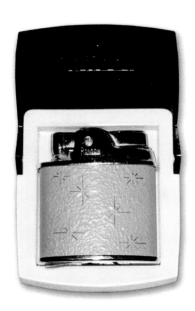

The "Sport" chromium and leather in a gift box, made by Ronson. Circa 1956. 2"h, 1¾"w. **$35.00 – 60.00.**

Chrome pocket lighter, made by Thornes. Circa late 1940s. 2½"h, 1¼"w. **$50.00 – 75.00.**

Pocket Lighters

The "Vara Flame" chromium butane pocket lighter with gift box, made by Ronson in England. Circa early 1960s. 2¾"h, 1" dia. at base. **$30.00 – 40.00.**

Chromium and leather pocket lighter that had to be handwound to operate. (Front and back shown.) Made by Henry Automatic. Circa mid 1920s. 2½"h, 1¾"w. **$80.00 – 110.00.**

Brass pocket lighter shaped like a book. Circa 1918. 2½"h, 1¾"w. **$100.00 – 125.00.**

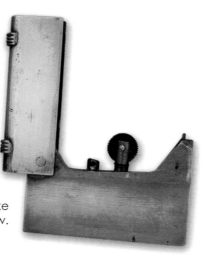

Chrome "Gem" pocket lighter, made by Ronson. Circa 1937. 2"h, 1¼"w. **$20.00 – 30.00.**

Zippo's D-Day Allied Heroes Collectors Edition set in a tin. This set has four brass-finished lighters with a key chain in the center. Circa 1994. Lighters, 2¼"h, 1½"w.; key chain, 1¼"dia.; tin, 2"h, 8"dia. **$100.00 – 125.00.**

Close-up view of General B.L. Montgomery.

Close-up view of General Omar Bradley.

Close-up view of General Dwight D. Eisenhower.

Close-up view of General Charles DeGaulle.

Pocket Lighters

Chromium pocket lighter (small flat center opens to light, a unique operation), made by Colby. Circa 1935. 2⅜"h, 1⅛"w. **$90.00 – 110.00.**

Chromium pocket lighter, made by Speed. Circa 1938. 2⅛"h, 1⅞"w. **$75.00 – 90.00.**

Chrome pocket lighter, made by Evans. Circa late 1920s. 2"h, 1½"w. **$50.00 – 70.00.**

Gold-tone with mother of pearl pocket lighter, made by Wiesner. Circa early 1950s.1½"h, 1½"w. **$30.00 – 45.00.**

Chrome "Banker" pocket lighter, made by Ronson. Circa late 1930s. 2¼"h, 1½"w. **$40.00 – 60.00.**

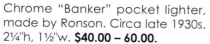

Chromium pocket lighter, made by Thorens. "Pat. Nov. 16, 1920". Circa 1921. 1⅞"h, 1⅛"w. **$50.00 – 75.00.**

Gold-tone pocket lighter, made by Evans. Circa mid 1930s. 2"h, 1½"w. **$70.00 – 90.00.**

Chromium with red leather insert band, made by Evans. Circa 1934. 2"h, 1½"w. **$25.00 – 40.00.**

Gold-tone and enamel pocket lighter, made by Evans. Circa 1930s. 2"h, 1½"w. **$75.00 – 100.00.**

Pocket Lighters

Brass and silver-plated basketweave design pocket lighter, by Evans. Circa 1934. 1½"h, 1½"w. **$40.00 – 60.00.**

Chrome and enamel pocket lighter with a wind guard, made by Evans. Circa 1930s. 2½"h, 1⅜"w. **$150.00 – 200.00.**

Chromium lift arm with leather band, made by Napier in France. Circa late 1930s. 1⅞"h, 1¾"w. **$80.00 – 100.00.**

Chrome and enamel pocket lighter, made by Wiesner. Circa 1950s. 2"h, 1⅝"w. **$25.00 – 50.00.**

Chromium and enamel pocket lighter with unique center slide operation (press the stem in), made by D.P.R. in Germany. Circa 1929. 1¾"h, 2¼"w. **$110.00 – 140.00.**

Chrome with clear plastic body pocket lighter, made by DuoLiter. Circa 1960s. 2⅝"h, 1¼"w. **$30.00 – 50.00.**

Brass and mother of pearl pocket lighter, made by Evans. Circa 1930s. 1½"h, 1½"w. **$50.00 – 70.00.**

The "Junior" chrome pocket lighter, made by Ronson. Circa late 1920s. 1⅝"h, 1½"w. **$75.00 – 100.00.**

Chromium lift arm pocket lighter with leather band (has a place for engraving initials), made by Golden Wheel. Circa 1928. 1¾"h, 1⅝"w. **$60.00 – 80.00.**

Chrome pocket lighter, made by Evans. Circa late 1920s. 2"h, 1½"w. **$75.00 – 100.00.**

Pocket Lighters

Brass pocket lighter with a leather band, made by Evans. Circa 1934. 1½"h, 1½"w. **$30.00 – 45.00.**

Brass with leather band pocket lighter, made by Evans. Circa late 1930s. 2"h, 1½"w. **$65.00 – 90.00.**

Gold-tone pocket lighter, made by Evans. Circa mid 1930s. 2"h, 1⅞"w. **$30.00 – 50.00.**

Gold-plated pocket lighter, made by Evans. Circa 1934. 2"h, 1½"w. **$40.00 – 60.00.**

Gold-tone with mother of pearl pocket lighter, made by Evans. Circa 1930s. 2"h, 1½"w. **$75.00 – 100.00.**

Sterling silver pocket lighter, made by D.P.R. in Germany. Circa early 1930s. 1⅞"h, 1½"w. **$90.00 – 110.00.**

Chromium and leather lift arm pocket lighter with built-in watch, made by Triangle. Circa 1928. 1¾"h, 1¾"w. **$250.00 – 300.00.**

Chrome pocket lighter, made by Evans. Circa 1930s. 2½"h, 1½"w. **$100.00 – 125.00.**

Chrome pocket lighter, made by Evans. Circa late 1930s. 2"h, 1½"w. **$50.00 – 70.00.**

The "Ace" pocket lighter, made by Ronson. Circa mid 1930s. 2"h, 1¾"w. **$75.00 – 100.00.**

Pocket Lighters

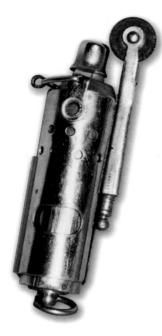

Chromium trench style pocket lighter, made in Austria. Circa 1918. 3"h, 1"w. **$30.00 – 50.00.**

Trench style pocket lighters. Both circa 1918. (a) Chromium. 2⅞"h, 1"w. (b) Brass. 2⅞"h, 1"w. **$30.00 – 50.00 each.**

Chrome lift arm pocket lighter with a diamond shaped watch made by Golden Wheel. Circa late 1920s. 2½"h, 1½"w. **$250.00 – 300.00.**

Chromium and tortoise enamel lift arm pocket lighter with gift box. Circa late 1920s. 1⅞"h, 1½"w. **$90.00 – 110.00.**

Silver-plated lift arm lighter with a watch, made in USA. Circa late 1920s. 2"h, 1⅜"w. **$250.00 – 300.00.**

Chromium and leather pocket lighter (has an eye viewer in the center that has risqué photos), made in Japan by Globe. Circa mid 1930s. 1⅞"h, 1½"w. **$100.00 – 125.00.**

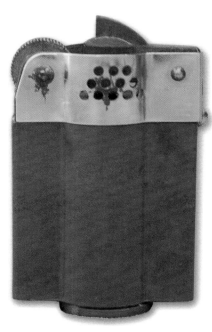

Chromium and leather lift arm pocket lighter, made by Triangle. Circa late 1920s. 1⅞"h, 1½"w. **$60.00 – 80.00.**

Chrome and Bakelite pocket lighter, made in England. Circa 1930s. 2¼"h, 1⅜"w. **$70.00 – 90.00.**

Chrome and mother of pearl pocket lighter, made in Germany. Circa 1930. 1¾"h, 1¾"w. **$150.00 – 200.00.**

Pocket Lighters

Brass pocket lighter with screw off wick cover (cover removed). Circa late 1910s. 2⅛"h, 1½"w. **$60.00 – 80.00.**

Chromium lift arm pocket lighter, made by Evans. Circa late 1920s. 2⅛"h, 1½"w. **$35.00 – 50.00.**

Unique metal and leather lift arm pocket lighter, made in Germany. Circa 1920. 1⅝"h, 1¾"w. **$125.00 – 150.00.**

Early "Duplex" pocket lighter in chromium and enamel (leather band missing), made by Ronson. Circa 1929. 2½"h, 1½"w. **$80.00 – 110.00.**

Chrome pocket knife with a built in lighter, finger nail file, and scissors, made in Japan. Circa 1950s. ⅞"h, 7"w opened; ⅞"h, 2¾"w closed. **$50.00 – 75.00.**

Silver pocket lighter. When the lid is raised, the lighter insert raises at the same time. Circa mid 1930s. 2¼"h, 1⅛"w. **$200.00 – 225.00.**

Brass and steel pocket lighter, made in Germany by D.P.R. Circa 1922. 2½"h, ⅞"w. **$50.00 – 75.00.**

Chrome mechanical pencil with the lighter built in at the top. Push the pocket clip to light. Made by Knight. Circa late 1940s. ¾"h, 5¼"w. **$30.00 – 50.00.**

Chromium pocket or table lighter, made by Evans. Circa 1934. 2"h, 1⅞"w. **$25.00 – 35.00.**

Chromium and leather lift arm with a built-in windshield, made by Golden Wheel. Circa late 1920s. 2⅛"h, 1¾"w. **$60.00 – 80.00.**

Pocket Lighters

Gold-tone pen liter. Top pulls off to reveal the lighter. Made by Hollywood Creations in New York City. Circa 1950s. ½"h, 5"w. **$20.00 – 30.00.**

Silver lift arm with a leather band and a built-in windscreen, made by Dunhill. Circa 1912. 2⅛"h, 1¾"w. **$275.00 – 325.00.**

Chrome pocket lighter with built in windscreen, made by Demely. Circa 1930s. 2"h, 1½"w. **$35.00 – 70.00.**

"Gem" chromium with leather band lift arm pocket lighters, made by Rex Mfg. Co. Circa 1930s. 2"h, 1⅜"w. **$35.00 – 50.00 each.**

Chrome and enamel pocket lighter, made by Omscolite. Circa late 1930s. 1⅞"h, 1⅝"w. **$30.00 – 50.00.**

Chrome pocket lighter with a working roulette wheel, made by Montecarlo. Circa 1950s. 2"h, 1⅝"w. **$25.00 – 40.00.**

A unique lift arm pocket lighter made in chromium and leather by Marathon. Circa 1925. 2"h, 1½"w. **$80.00 – 110.00.**

Matte finished pocket lighter with laser engraving of the New Jersey State P.B.A. insignia, made by Zippo. Circa 1990s. 2¼"h, 1½"w. **$30.00 – 50.00.**

Pocket Lighters

Aluminum and painted pocket lighter, made by Warner. Circa late 1930s. 1⅞"h, 1½"w. **$75.00 – 100.00.**

18 karat gold electroplated lift arm pocket lighter with a leather band, made by Clark. "Pat. July 27, 1926." Circa 1927. 1⅞"h, 1½"w. **$60.00 – 85.00.**

Gold-plated pocket lighter with gift box, instructions, and cleaning brush, made by Evans. Circa 1934. 2"h, 1½"w. **$75.00 – 90.00.**

Chromium and brass lift arm pocket lighter. Circa late 1920s. 2⅛"h, 1½"w. **$35.00 – 50.00.**

Chromium pocket lighter, made by Evans. Circa 1929. 2"h, 1½"w. **$50.00 – 70.00.**

Early chromium pocket lighter, made by Thorens. Circa mid 1930s. 2⅛"h, 1½"w. **$40.00 – 60.00.**

Chromium pocket lighter, made by Thorens. Circa early 1930s. 2⅛"h, 1½"w. **$50.00 – 70.00.**

Chromium pocket lighter with a leather band. Circa 1930s. 1¾"h, 1½"w. **$50.00 – 70.00.**

Chromium and leather pocket lighter that has a different type of lighting mechanism, made by Morton. Circa mid 1930s. 2"h, 1⅝"w. **$80.00 – 100.00.**

Chromium and leather lift arm pocket lighter made by Superfine. Circa early 1930s. 1⅞"h, 1½"w. **$75.00 – 100.00.**

Pocket Lighters

Gold-plated lift arm pocket lighter, made by Rexlite. Circa late 1920s. 1¾"h, 1½"w. **$75.00 – 100.00.**

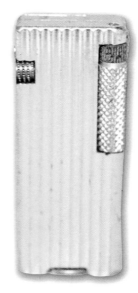
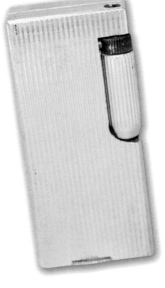

Chromium lift arm pocket lighters. (a) Made by Sharpo. Circa 1935. 2⅜"h, ⅞"w. **$35.00 – 50.00.** (b) Made by Cygnus. Circa 1928. 2½"h, 1"w. **$25.00 – 40.00.**

Brass and Bakelite pocket lighter with a unique lift arm for the Tenth Olympiad. Circa 1932. 2¼"h, 1¾"w. **$80.00 – 100.00.**

(a) Brass pocket lighter with German wording that translates to "God Is With Us." Circa 1918. 2⅝"h, 2"w. **$125.00 – 150.00.** (b) Small brass pocket lighter. Circa 1918. 2"h, 1½"w. **$50.00 – 75.00.**

Early chromium "Magic Pocket Lamp and Cigar Lighter" with gift box and tin for the flint disk. "Koopmans Pat. Oct. 29, 89 [sole mfrs] New York." Circa 1890. 2½"h, 1¾"w. **$225.00 – 275.00.**

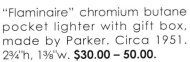

"Flaminaire" chromium butane pocket lighter with gift box, made by Parker. Circa 1951. 2¾"h, 1⅜"w. **$30.00 – 50.00.**

Chromium lift arm pocket lighter, made in England. Circa 1948. 1¾"h, 1¼"w. **$80.00 – 100.00.**

Pocket Lighters

Chromium pocket pipe lighter with gift box, made by Beattie. Circa early 1950s. 2⅛"h, 1¾"w. **$30.00 – 50.00.**

Chromium service lighter, made in England by Dunhill. Circa early 1940s. 2⁵⁄₁₆"h, 1⅛"w. **$35.00 – 50.00.**

Chromium musical pocket lighter, made by Prince. Circa 1960s. 2⅛"h, 1¾"w. **$30.00 – 50.00.**

"Adonis" blue enamel pocket lighter with ivory colored cherubs and a gift box, made by Ronson. Circa 1954. 1¾"h, 2⅛"w. **$40.00 – 60.00.**

"Capri" blue enamel pocket lighter with ivory colored cherubs and a gift box, made by Ronson. Circa 1954. 2⅛"h, 1¾"w. **$45.00 – 75.00.**

Chromium heart-shaped pocket lighter (plastic insert colored to simulate mother of pearl), made by Continental. Circa mid 1950s. 2"h, 2"w. **$15.00 – 25.00.**

Pouch style pocket lighter, made by Colibri. Circa 1954. 2⅛"h, 2"w. **$40.00 – 60.00.**

Chromium tube style pocket lighter. Circa late 1950s. 2⅜"h, ⅜" dia. **$5.00 – 15.00.**

Gold-plated lift arm pocket lighter made by Dunhill. Circa 1950s. 3"h, ⅞"w. **$225.00 – 275.00.**

Chromium double wick lighter made by Dub-L-Lite. Circa 1948. 2¼"h, 1½"w. **$40.00 – 50.00.**

Pocket Lighters

Chromium lift arm pocket lighter with a leather band, made by Continental. Circa late 1940s. 2⅛"h, 1½"w. **$65.00 – 90.00.**

Chromium and brass finish pocket lighter, made by Elgin American. Circa late 1940s. 1¾"h, 2⅛"w. **$25.00 – 40.00.**

"Adonis" pocket lighters made by Ronson. Circa late 1947. (a) Chromium and black enamel. 1⅞"h, 2⅛"w. **$25.00 – 40.00.** (b) Silver-plated. 1⅞"h, 2⅛"w. **$40.00 – 50.00.**

Brass with ivory colored band, made by Pigeon. Circa early 1960s. 1⅜"h, 1¾"w. **$20.00 – 30.00.**

Chromium butane pocket lighter, made by Strato Flame. Circa 1952. 1¾"h, 2¼"w. **$25.00 – 40.00.**

Gold-plated musical pocket lighter with gift box, plays "Home on the Range" made by CROWN. Circa late 1940s. 2⅝"h, 1¾"w. **$60.00 – 80.00.**

Chromium pocket lighter with changeable calendar. Circa early 1960s. 2¼"h, 1½"w. **$30.00 – 40.00.**

Chromium butane pocket lighter with view finder, gift box, and instructions, made by Royale. Circa late 1950s. 1⅛"h, 2⅝"w. **$30.00 – 40.00.**

Silver-plated butane lift arm pocket lighter with gift box, made in England by Dunhill. Circa 1990. 2½"h, 1⅛"w. **$225.00 – 250.00.**

Box of twelve chromium and black enamel service lighters, made by Dunhill. Circa early 1940s. 2⅜"h, 1"w. **$40.00 – 50.00 each.**

Pocket Lighters

Chromium pocket service lighter made by Parker. Circa early 1940s. 2⁵⁄₁₆"h, 1¹⁄₁₆" w. **$35.00 – 50.00.**

Chromium pocket lighters made by Ronson. (a) "Standard." Circa early 1950s. 2"h, 1¾"w. **$15.00 – 25.00.** (b) "Whirlwind." Circa 1941. 2⅛"h, 1¾"w. **$25.00 – 40.00.** (c) "Princess." Circa early 1950s. 2"h, 1½"w. **$15.00 – 25.00.**

Chromium lift arm replica pocket lighter with gift box, made by Colibri. Circa 1986. 2⅝"h, 1¼"w. **$65.00 – 80.00.**

"Varaflame" chromium butane pocket lighter with gift box, made by Ronson. Circa 1960s. 2¾"h, 1"w. **$30.00 – 40.00.**

Chromium pocket lighters made by Ronson. (a) "Standard." Circa early 1950s. 2⅛"h, 1½"w. **$15.00 – 25.00.** (b) "Whirlwind." Circa 1941. 2⅛"h, 1¾"w. **$35.00 – 50.00.**

Chromium pocket lighter with box and instructions, made by Nimrod. Circa early 1970s. 3⅛"h, ¾"w. **$25.00 – 40.00.**

Brass cylinder painted blue and black, made by BALLoFLINT. Circa late 1940s. 2⅝"h, ½" dia. **$20.00 – 30.00.**

Brass musical pocket lighter plays "On the Atchison, Topeka, and the Santa Fe," made by CROWN. Circa late 1940s. 2⅝"h, 1⅜"w. **$75.00 – 90.00.**

Chromium pocket lighter with a watch, made by Eclydo Co. (Note: Watch has a small second hand.) Circa early 1950s. 2½ h, 1⅝"w. **$125.00 – 150.00.**

Brass heart-shaped pocket lighter with gift box, cloth pouch, cleaning brush, and instructions, made by Elgin American. Circa early 1950s. 2⅛"h, 2⅜"w. **$80.00 – 100.00.**

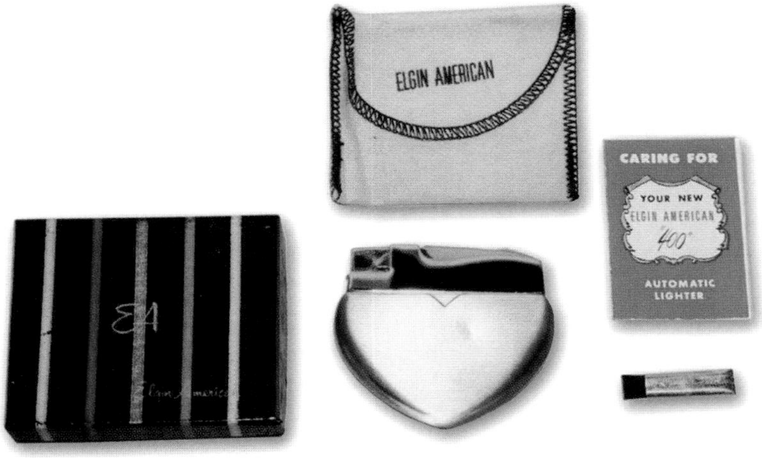

Pocket Lighters

Gold-plated musical pocket lighter, made by Crown (plays "Smoke Gets in Your Eyes"). Circa late 1940s. 2⅝"h, 2"w. **$60.00 – 85.00.**

The "Flaminare" chromium and enamel pocket lighter, made by Parker Pen Co. Circa mid 1950s. 2¾"h, 1⅜"w. **$20.00 – 40.00.**

Chromium butane pocket lighter, made by Tanra Mfg. Co. Circa mid 1950s. 2¼"h, 1⅜"w. **$20.00 – 30.00.**

A unique brass lift arm, lever action pocket lighter. Circa 1918. 1⅜"h, ⅞"w. **$200.00 – 250.00.**

Gold-plated pocket lighter with gift box, made by Evans. Circa late 1930s. 2"h, 1⅞"w. **$60.00 – 80.00.**

The "Lucky" chromium pocket lighter with a unique lift arm and a built-in windscreen, made by Thorens. Circa mid 1930s. 2"h, 1½"w. **$125.00 – 150.00.**

Silver plate with leaf etched pattern, made by Zippo. Circa 1994. 2¼"h, 1½"w. **$60.00 – 75.00.**

Gold-plated lift arm pocket lighter with a wooden gift box. This is a replica of the 1928 model, made by Colibri. Circa 1994. 1⅞"h, 1⅜"w. **$90.00 – 115.00.**

Chromium pocket lighter, made by Evans. Circa 1934. 2"h, 1½"w. **$25.00 – 40.00.**

Chromium lift arm pocket lighter, made by Polo in England. Circa 1932. 1¾"h, 1½"w. **$85.00 – 110.00.**

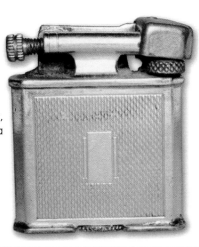

Chromium pocket lighter, made by Colibri. Circa mid 1950s. 1¾"h, 1⅝"w. **$40.00 – 60.00.**

Pocket Lighters

Gold-plated pocket lighter on a display stand, made by Elgin American. Circa mid 1950s. 1¼"h, 2⅛"w. **$60.00 – 85.00.**

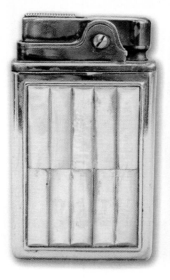

Gold-plated with mother of pearl musical pocket lighter, made by PAC. Circa early 1950s. 2⅝"h, 1⅜"w. **$90.00 – 115.00.**

Chromium lift arm pocket lighter, made by Polo in England. Circa 1932. 2⅛"h, 1⅝"w. **$75.00 – 100.00.**

"His and Hers" chromium set of pocket lighters in a gift box, made by Ronson. Circa 1955. Left lighter, 2"h, 1⅜"w; right lighter, 2⅛"h, 2⅝"w. **$90.00 – 115.00.**

Chromium butane pocket lighter, made by Colibri. Circa mid 1970s. 2½"h, ⅞"w. **$25.00 – 40.00.**

Chromium lift arm pocket lighter with a watch (watch has a separate second hand), made by Malton. Circa late 1920s. 2"h, 1⅜"w. **$225.00 – 275.00.**

Electro-Quartz chromium with leather accent butane pocket lighter, made by Colibri. Circa 1960s. 3"h, 1"w. **$75.00 – 100.00.**

Gift set, lighter has an antique copper finish, also included are spare flints and lighter fluid, made by Zippo. Circa 1994. Lighter is 2¼"h, 1½"w. **$25.00 – 35.00.**

The "Comet" chromium and plastic butane pocket lighter, made by Ronson. Circa late 1950s. 2¼"h, 1½"w. **$10.00 – 15.00.**

Pocket Lighters

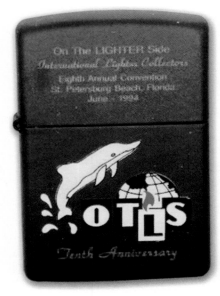

O.T.L.S. Lighter Club's 10th anniversary lighter has a mat black finish, made by Zippo. Circa 1994. 2¼"h, 1½"w. **$30.00 – 40.00.**

The "Gem" chromium finish with rhinestones, made by Ronson. Circa 1937. 2"h, 1¼"w. **$100.00 – 125.00.**

The "Cadet" chromium pocket lighter, made by Ronson in England. Circa 1959. 2⅛"h, 1¾"w. **$30.00 – 45.00.**

Silver butane pocket lighter, made by Cartier in France. Circa late 1970s. 2¾"h, 1"w. **$150.00 – 175.00.**

Chromium butane pocket lighter, made by Bentley. Circa mid 1950s. 1½"h, 2⅛"w. **$10.00 – 20.00.**

Gold-plated and black enamel "Literpact," made by Ronson. (Compact in the center with a mirror.) Circa 1938. 2 ⅞"h, 2 ⅜"w. **$150.00 – 200.00.**

Same as lighter on left only in chromium and ivory enamel finish.

Gold-plated lift arm pocket lighter, made by Dunhill in England. Circa 1934. 2½"h, ⅞"w. **$225.00 – 275.00.**

Sets

Glass and brass two-piece set made by Evans. Circa 1950s. Lighter, 5½"h, 2⅝" dia.; ashtray, 2⅛"h, 3⅞" dia. **$75.00 – 100.00.**

Green ceramic two-piece set made by Evans. Circa mid 1950s. Lighter, 2½"h, 4"w; ashtray, 1½"h, 4½"w. **$30.00 – 40.00.**

Brass decorative cigarette box and lighter made by Evans. Circa late 1930s. Lighter, 5"h, 2¼"w; box, 3½"h, 5 ⅜"w. **$75.00 – 100.00.**

Two-piece Lucite set with ocean scene made by Evans. Circa 1950s. Lighter, 3½"h, 3"w; clock, 4¼"h, 5⅞"w. **$125.00 – 150.00.**

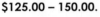

Five-piece set made by Evans. Circa 1950s. Lighter, 3½"h, 2¼"w; ashtrays, ½"h, 3" dia. **$80.00 – 100.00.**

Six-piece Lenox china set with Ronson lighter insert. Circa early 1960s. Llighter, 4¼"h, 2¾"w; cigarette holder, 4"h, 2¾"w; ashtrays, ⅝"h, 4¼"w. **$100.00 – 125.00.**

The "Cornucopia" set made by Evans. Circa mid 1950s. Lighter, 4"h, 5"w; cigarette holder, 3¼"h, 4⅞"w. **$150.00 – 175.00.**

Three-piece Lucite set made by Evans. Circa early 1950s. Lighter, 3"h, 4½"w; candle holders, 2¼"h, 2"w. **$80.00 – 100.00.**

Wedgewood lighter and ashtray made by Evans. This set is from the estate of Ginger Rogers. Circa late 1940s. Lighter, 2½"h, 2¼"w; ashtray, ½"h, 3¾" dia. **$150.00 – 200.00.**

Ceramic lighter and ashtray made by Evans. Circa early 1950s. Lighter, 3"h, 2½"w; ashtray, ¾"h, 4½" dia. **$75.00 – 90.00**

Sets

Two-piece Lucite set with pheasants, made by Evans. Circa mid 1950s. Lighter, 3"h, 3"w; pen holder, ¾"h, 3⅛"w. **$75.00 – 100.00.**

Two-piece ceramic set (with snowy cabin scene on both pieces) made by Evans. Circa early 1950s. Lighter, 3⅞"h, 2½"w; ashtray, ¾"h, 4⅝"w. **$75.00 – 100.00.**

Four-piece brass and imitation pearl set made by Evans. Circa 1950s. Lighter, 1½"h, 1½"w; cigarette case, 3"h, 3⅞"w; compact, 2¼"h, 2⅞"w; lipstick, 2⅛"h, ¾"w. **$100.00 – 125.00.**

Two-piece enameled set made by Evans. Circa early 1950s. Lighter, 2"h, 1½"w; compact, ⅜"h, 2½" dia. **$100.00 – 150.00.**

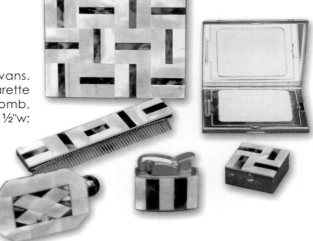

Six-piece mother of pearl set made by Evans. Circa late 1930s. Lighter, 1½"h, 1½"w; cigarette case, 3"h, 4"w; compact, 2½"h, 2¾"w; comb, ¾"h, 4¼"w; lipstick with fold out mirrors, 3"h, 1½"w; pill box, 1¼"h, 1¼"w. **$350.00 – 450.00.**

Two-piece enameled set made by Evans. Circa late 1940s. Cigarette case, 3"h, 3⅞"w; compact, 2½"h, 2½"w. **$80.00 – 100.00.** **Sets**

Five-piece set in brass and ceramic made by Evans. Circa early 1950s. Lighter, 6¾"h, 2½"w; cigarette holders, 2½"h, 2⅜" dia.; ashtrays, 1¼"h, 5½" dia. **$75.00 – 100.00.**

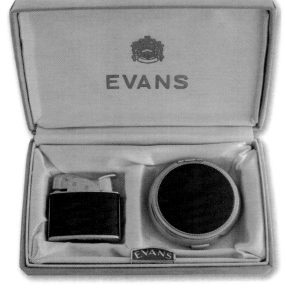

Two-piece set with raised enamel finish, made by Evans. Circa late 1940s. Lighter, 1½"h, 1½"w; compact, ½"h, 3" dia. **$75.00 – 100.00.**

Two-piece set made by Evans. Circa 1950s. Lighter, 1½"h, 1½"w; case, 2⅛"h, 2¾"w. **$75.00 – 100.00.**

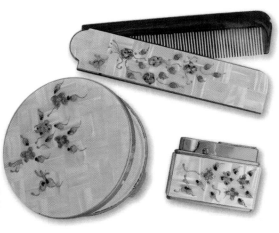

Three-piece mother of pearl set with raised jeweled floral design, made in Japan. Circa 1950s. Lighter, 1¼"h, 1¾"w; comb, 1"h, 4"w; compact, ½"h, 2¾" dia. **$80.00 – 100.00.**

Sets

Brass basketweave design two-piece set made by Evans. Circa 1930s. Lighter, 2"h, 1¾"w; compact, 2¼"h, 3⅛"w. **$90.00 – 120.00.**

Brass with painted figural scene, made by Evans. Circa early 1950s. Lighter, 1½"h, 1½"w; compact, ⅝"h, 1¾" dia. **$100.00 – 125.00.**

Three-piece brass and mother of pearl set made by Elgin America. Circa late 1940s. Lighter, 1⅝"h, 2⅛"w; cigarette case, 2¾"h, 4"w; compact, 2¼"h, 2½"w. **$75.00 – 100.00.**

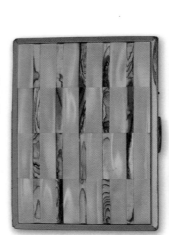
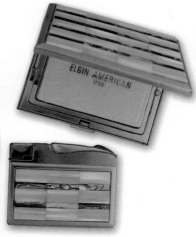

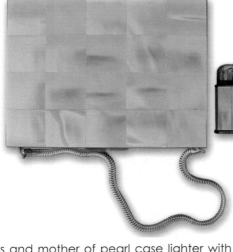
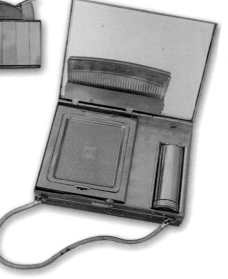

Brass and mother of pearl case lighter with compact and cigarette case, made by Evans. Circa 1930s. Lighter, 1½"h, 1½"w; compact, 3"h, 4"w. **$100.00 – 125.00.**

Two-piece lighter and cigarette case set in brass and multicolored enamel finish, made by Evans. Circa late 1930s. Lighter, 1½"h, 1½"w; case, 1¾"h, 3¾"w. **$40.00 – 60.00.**

Two-piece chrome and enamel lighter with cigarette case, made by Evans. Circa mid 1930s. Lighter, 2"h, 1¼"w; case, 4"h, 2⅞"w. **$80.00 – 100.00.**

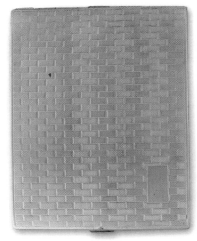

Chrome with basketweave design lighter and case, made by Evans. Circa mid 1930s. Lighter, 2"h, 1¼"w; case, 3¾"h, 2⅞"w. **$100.00 – 125.00.**

Four-piece ceramic table lighter set made by Evans. Circa mid 1930s. Lighter, 6⅞"h, 2½"w; cigarette box, 3"h, 4¼"w; ashtrays, 1"h, 4⅛"dia. **$100.00 – 125.00.**

Brass lighter and compact made by Evans. Circa late 1930s. Lighter, 1½"h, 1½"w; compact, 2½"h, 2½"w. **$75.00 – 100.00.**

Sets

Ceramic and brass table set made by Evans. Circa 1930s. Lighter, 2⅝"h, 2¼" dia.; ashtrays, 2¼"h, 3"w. **$75.00 – 100.00.**

Chrome two-piece set made by Evans. Circa late 1920s. Lighter, 2"h, 1½"w; case, 2⅞"h, 3⅞"w. **$125.00 – 150.00.**

Brass two-piece lighter set made by Evans. Circa 1930s. Lighter, 1½"h, 1½"w; compact, 3"h, 5⅜"w. **$100.00 – 125.00.**

Four-piece brass and enamel dress set made by Evans. Circa early 1950s. Lighter, 2"h, 1½"w; cuff links, 1"h, ⅝"w; tie bar, ½"h, 1⅝"w. **$75.00 – 100.00.**

Gold-tone two-piece lighter set with compact that has a built-in watch, made by Evans. Circa early 1930s. Lighter, 1½"h, 1½"w; compact, 2½"h, 2½"w. **$150.00 – 200.00.**

Limited edition chrome and mother of pearl lighter and knife set. Lighter made by Zippo, knife made by Case, in a wooden engraved box. Circa late 1990s. Lighter, 2¼"h, 1½"w; knife (closed), ¾"h, 3¼"w. **$400.00 – 500.00.**

Metal and leather lighter and case (slide to open the top case) made by Park Sherman. Circa 1940s. Lighter, 2⅛"h, 1½"w; case, 2⅞"h, 2¼"w. **$75.00 – 100.00.**

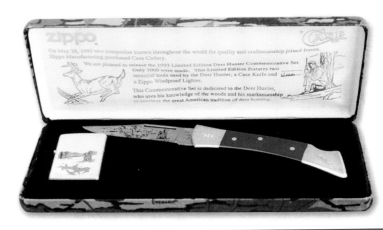

Limited edition lighter and knife set, made by Zippo and Case. Circa 1993. Lighter, 2¼"h, 1½"w; knife opened, 1¼"h, 8⅜"w. **$425.00 – 525.00.**

Three-piece chromium table lighter set with plastic handles, made by A.S.R. Circa early 1950s. Lighter, 3"h, 4¾"w; cigarette holder, 2¼"h, 4¾"w; tray, 5¾" x 9½". **$75.00 – 90.00.**

"Queen Anne" two-piece set made by Ronson. Circa 1936. Lighter, 2⅝"h, 3⅛"w; cigarette holder, 2⅞"h, 2½"dia. **$45.00 – 75.00.**

Three-piece ceramic set made by Evans. Circa 1940s. Lighter, 7"h, 3"dia.; ashtray, 1⅜"h, 5½"w; cigarette box, 1¾"h, 4"w. **$75.00 – 100.00.**

Two-piece black marble and chromium "Nordic" set made by Ronson. Circa 1955. Lighter, 3"h, 2¾" dia.; cigarette holder, 2⅞"h, 2¼"dia. **$30.00 – 60.00.**

Brass, white and clear Lucite plastic three-piece set, made by Evans. (Each-piece has a picture of a rainbow trout decorating it.) Circa early 1950s. Lighter, 3½"h, 2⅝"w; cigarette box, 1¾"h, 4¼"w; pen holder, ¾"h, 3¼"w. **$100.00 – 125.00.**

Ceramic with brass trim three-piece set made by Stylebuilt Accessories. Circa early 1950s. Lighter, 3¾"h, 3⅛"w; ashtray, 1¼"h, 3¾" dia.; cigarette holder, 2¾"h, 3⅛"w. **$60.00 – 70.00.**

Lighter is ceramic lamp and cat on a book (the pull chain operates the lighter). The center of the wooden box is open to see where the cigarettes are held and the ashtray is recessed on the right side, also has a built-in music box, made by Venus. Circa late 1930s. 7¾"h, 11¾"w. **$125.00 – 150.00.**

Brass and plastic table lighter with stand and four ashtrays made by A.S.R. Circa late 1940s. Lighter, 2¾"h, 1⅞"w; ashtrays, 3" dia. **$45.00 – 60.00.**

Brass and ceramic with gold trim two-piece set made by Evans. Circa late 1930s. Lighter, 3"h, 3¾"w; cigarette holder, 2⅜"h, 3¾"w. **$70.00 – 90.00.**

Three-piece ceramic with gold trim, made by Evans. Circa late 1930s. Lighter, 2"h, 3" dia.; cigarette holder, 2"h, 3" dia.; ashtray, 1"h, 3" dia. **$50.00 – 60.00.**

Sets

Chromium and enamel lift arm lighter with cigarette case in a gift box, made by Girey. Circa 1935. Lighter, 1¾"h, 1½"w; cigarette case, 3⅛"h, 4¼"w. **$80.00 – 100.00.**

Chromium brush finish with gold trim two-piece set made by Evans. Circa mid 1950s. Lighter, 4½"h, 2¼" dia.; ashtray, 1"h, 6" dia. **$50.00 – 75.00.**

Brass and leather covered case made by Evans. Circa mid 1930s. 1½"h, 6¼"w. **$40.00 – 60.00.**

Ceramic two-piece set made of Delft glass. Circa 1930s. Lighter and ashtray each, 1½"h, 3¼"w. **$40.00 – 70.00.**

Two-piece brass and enamel set made by Evans. Circa late 1950s. Lighter, 4"h, 3" dia.; cigarette holder, 2¼"h, 2¼" dia. **$50.00 – 75.00.**

Zebra leg with a custom fit Ronson lighter. Circa mid 1970s. 14"h, 7" dia. at base. **$150.00 – 200.00.**

Deer hoof with a brass finished lighter. Circa 1960s. 3¼"h, 5¼"w. **$100.00 – 125.00.**

Lucite lighter with a chrome bulldog, made by Evans. Circa mid 1950s. 3¼"h, 1⅞"w. **$30.00 – 40.00.**

Lucite lighter with a rose, made by Evans. Circa mid 1950s. 3"h, 2"w. **$30.00 – 40.00.**

Chesterfield cigarette package in Lucite, made by Evans. Circa mid 1950s. 3¼"h, 1⅞"w. **$30.00 – 40.00.**

Table Lighters

Pheasant in Lucite, made by Evans. Circa mid 1950s. 3¼"h, 2"w. **$30.00 – 40.00.**

Metal phonograph musical lighter, made by Swank (record turns when lighter is lit). Circa 1950s. 6½"h, 3¾"w. **$50.00 – 60.00.**

Silent Flame table lighter, uses batteries and fluid. Made by Dunhill. Circa late 1940s. 2½"h, 3"w. **$75.00 – 90.00.**

Egg-shaped lighter, made by Evans. Circa mid 1950s. 2½"h, 3"w. **$60.00 – 75.00.**

Ceramic lady table lighter, made in Japan. Circa 1950s. 4"h, 2¼"w. **$25.00 – 40.00.**

Brass table lighter with a clock. The lighter is in the shape of a gas pump that is lit by using the flint striker that is the nozzle on the hose of the pump. Also has a built-in changeable calendar. Made in Germany. Circa 1950s. 4½"h, 7"w. **$125.00 – 150.00.**

Brass and painted cigar store Indian, made by Evans. Circa late 1940s. 8"h, 2½"w. **$200.00 – 250.00.**

Golf bag on cart in chrome and red paint, made in Japan. To light, pull the handle on the cart. Circa late 1960s. 5¼"h, 4"w. **$50.00 – 75.00.**

Glass table lighter with pheasant, made by Evans. Circa 1950s. 5½"h, 2¼" dia. **$50.00 – 75.00.**

Glass table lighter with Canadian goose, made by Evans. Circa 1950s. 5½"h, 2¼" dia. **$50.00 – 75.00.**

Table Lighters

Chrome and tortoise Lucite table lighter, made by Thornes. Circa late 1940s. 3¾"h, 1¾"w. **$50.00 – 75.00.**

Small mother of pearl table lighter, made by Evans. Circa 1950s. 2"h, 2"w. **$40.00 – 60.00.**

Chrome table lighter, made by Dunhill. Circa late 1940s. 3½"h, 2⅛" dia. **$200.00 – 250.00.**

Brass covered wagon table lighter, made by Evans. Circa 1940s. 3"h, 3¾"w. **$50.00 – 70.00.**

Brass and painted table lighter with moveable hands on the face of the clock and changeable message, also has the international time zones on the base, made by Swank. Circa 1930s. 8¾"h, 2¼"w. **$75.00 – 100.00.**

Ceramic lighter, made in France, from the estate of actress Ginger Rogers. Circa late 1930s. 2½"h, 1½" dia. **$100.00 – 150.00.**

Small Bakelite table lighter shaped like a bottle of nail polish, made by Strikalite. Circa 1930s. 2⅜"h, 1"w. **$20.00 – 30.00.**

Metal and Bakelite table lighter, made by Emson. Circa 1930s. 2⅞"h, 3⅝"w. **$50.00 – 75.00.**

Table Lighters

Chrome and copper finish "Regal" table lighters, made by Ronson. Circa mid 1950s. 2¼"h, 3¼"w. **$25.00 – 50.00 each.**

Chrome "Queen Anne" table lighter, made by Ronson. Circa 1936. 2⅝"h, 3⅛"w. **$25.00 – 40.00.**

Chrome and Bakelite table clock with built-in striker lighter, made by Match King. Circa late 1920s. 4"h, 5¾"w. **$150.00 – 200.00.**

Brass Statue of Liberty lighter on a Bakelite base, made in USA. Flame comes out of torch. Circa 1930s. 8"h, 3⅝"w at base. **$75.00 – 100.00.**

Metal lift arm nude figural table lighter. Circa mid 1920s. 6¼"h, 3"w. **$75.00 – 100.00.**

Butane chrome golfer table lighter, made in Japan. When lit the golfer swings at the ball. 3"h, 3¼"w. **$35.00 – 50.00.**

Chrome alarm clock table lighter, made in Japan. To light, push in the bell. Circa 1950s. 2½"h, 1⅞"w. **$70.00 – 90.00.**

Brass butane torch table lighter, made by Pyro Star. Circa mid 1960s. 5"h, 4¾"w. **$30.00 – 50.00.**

Brass music box table lighter that turns the "two faced" man when lit, made by Evans. Circa late 1930s. 5½"h, 3½" dia. **$100.00 – 125.00.**

Silver lift arm 6" ruler table lighter, made by Dunhill. Circa mid 1930s. 6½"h, ¾"w. **$250.00 – 300.00.**

Table Lighters

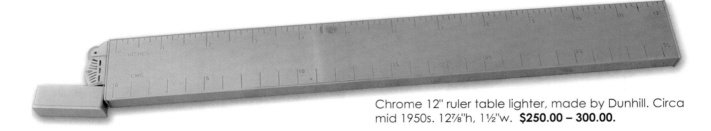

Chrome 12" ruler table lighter, made by Dunhill. Circa mid 1950s. 12⅞"h, 1½"w. **$250.00 – 300.00.**

Gold-tone 12" ruler table lighter, made by Penguin. Circa 1950s. 13"h, 1½"w. **$50.00 – 75.00.**

Silver-plated table lighter, made by Dunhill. Circa mid 1930s. 2⅝"h, 1¼"w. **$200.00 – 225.00.**

Painted wooden monk table lighter. Circa late 1930s. 6½"h, 2½"w. **$85.00 – 100.00.**

Chrome and marble-like lift arm table lighter, made by Dunhill. Circa late 1950s. 2⅞"h, 2¾"w. **$250.00 – 300.00.**

Chrome and leather electric/butane table lighter, made by Evans. Circa late 1950s. 2¾"h, 4"w. **$80.00 – 100.00.**

Chromium and gold-tone coffee pot table lighter, made in USA. Circa late 1930s. 3"h, 1¾"w. **$50.00 – 75.00.**

Silver-plated lift arm 12" ruler table lighter, made by Dunhill. Circa early 1930s. 12⅝"h, 1¼"w. **$300.00 – 500.00.**

Chrome and leather lift arm lighter, made in the USA. Circa 1920s. 3¾"h, 2⅛"w. **$75.00 – 125.00.**

Chrome table lighter with a windguard. Circa late 1930s. 3⅞"h, 3"w. **$75.00 – 100.00.**

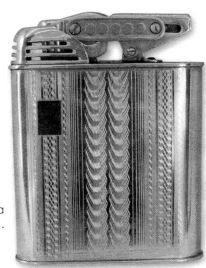

Table Lighters

Copper table lighter with black painted wooden handle, made by Ronson. Circa mid 1950s. 3⅜"h, 5¼"w. **$30.00 – 50.00.**

Chrome and enamel table lighter that looks like a grill to a Jaguar automobile (turn the Jaguar to light). Made in Japan. Circa 1968. 4⅛"h, 3¾"w. **$40.00 – 60.00.**

Gold-plated lift arm table lighter (when the lighter is set down the arm comes down over the wick to snuff out the flame), made by Segal. Circa late 1920s. 4"h, 1½"w. **$90.00 – 120.00.**

Chromium table lighter, made by Parker. Circa mid 1930s. 3"h, 1⅜"w. **$35.00 – 50.00.**

"Crown" quadruple silver-plated table lighter, made by Ronson. Circa 1936. 2¼"h, 2¾"w. **$45.00 – 60.00.**

"Georgian" silver-plated table lighter, made by Ronson. Circa 1936. 2½"h, 3¼"w. **$45.00 – 60.00.**

Brass and leather (made to look like a bucket) table lighter, by Evans. Circa mid 1930s. 4¼"h, 2¼"w. **$50.00 – 70.00.**

Brass table lighter with a leather base (has a unique thumb slide mechanism on the side), made by Evans. Circa mid 1930s. 2⅛"h, 2½" dia. **$60.00 – 75.00.**

Brass and fur covered table lighter, made by Evans. Circa 1934. 3"h, 1¾" dia. **$35.00 – 50.00.**

Chromium table lighter, made in England by Éclair. Circa mid 1930s. 4¼"h, 1½" dia. at base. **$100.00 – 120.00.**

Table Lighters

Chromium table lighter with leather band, made by The Giant. Circa early 1950s. 4"h, 3⅜"w. **$25.00 – 35.00.**

Chromium airplane table lighter (lights by turning the propeller). Circa 1935. 3⅛"h, 5¾"w, 7¼" wing span. **$110.00 – 140.00.**

Chromium and paint airplane table lighter (lights by turning the propeller). Circa 1935. 3"h, 6"w, 5" wing span. **$80.00 – 100.00.**

Brass table lighter, made by Capitol. "Patented Sept. 17, 1912." (Notice the many levers and springs to operate this lighter.) Circa 1913. 5"h, 2⅞" dia. at base. **$175.00 – 250.00.**

"Tabourette" chromium and leather table lighter, made by Ronson. Circa 1929. 4⅛"h, 2⅛"w. **$110.00 – 150.00.**

Metal and paint lift arm table lighter made by De-Lux. Circa 1928. 3⅞"h, 2¼"w. **$55.00 – 70.00.**

Chromium with leather covered base table lighter, made by Thorens. Circa 1938. 3¾"h, 1¾" dia. **$60.00 – 80.00.**

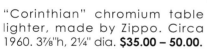

"Corinthian" chromium table lighter, made by Zippo. Circa 1960. 3⅞"h, 2¼" dia. **$35.00 – 50.00.**

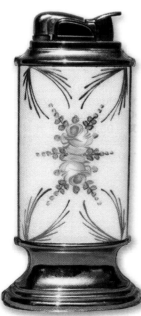

Chromium and enamel cylinder table lighter. Circa late 1940s. 3¼"h, 1⅞" dia. **$25.00 – 40.00.**

Brass and floral with gold trim table lighter, made by Evans. Circa late 1940s. 4⅞"h, 2¼"w. **$45.00 – 60.00.**

Table Lighters

Chromium ship wheel table lighter (lights by turning the wheel), made by Dunhill. Circa 1935. 5"h, 2⅞" dia. at base. **$175.00 – 250.00.**

"Nautical" touch tip ship wheel table lighter with bronze finish and copper wheel, made by Ronson. Circa 1939. 4¾"h, 3"w. **$225.00 – 300.00.**

Brass and leather lift arm table lighter, made in Japan by Nesor. Circa mid 1950s. 5¾"h, 3½"w. **$40.00 – 60.00.**

Brass table lighter, made by Park Sherman. Circa early 1960s. 2½"h, 1½"w. **$20.00 – 30.00.**

Brass candlestick holder and candle table lighter (lever on the right side above the finger hole handle operates the lighter at the top of the candle). Circa early 1920s. 5½"h, 3½"w at base. **$150.00 – 175.00.**

Chromium and blue marble-like plastic, made in Japan (unique lighter mechanism). Circa early 1950s. 3½"h, 1½" dia. at base. **$30.00 – 40.00.**

P – 51 Mustang chromium airplane table lighter, made by Negbaur in Germany (lights by turning the propeller). Circa 1948. 3"h, 6⅜"w, 6¼" wing span. **$90.00 – 115.00.**

Brass "Spirit of St. Louis" airplane with rubber tires, made by SWANK (lights by turning the propeller). Circa late 1940s. 1¾"h, 5⅜"w, 6⅝" wing span. **$100.00 – 125.00.**

Chromium ship wheel table lighter, made by Hamilton (lights by turning the wheel). Circa late 1930s. 5⅛"h, 2¾" dia. at base. **$75.00 – 100.00.**

Chromium table lighter, (lights when it is picked up). Circa mid 1950s. 2⅜"h, 3"w. **$20.00 – 30.00.**

Table Lighters

Metal and glass parlor lighter with wick snuffer in place. Circa 1860s. 4½"h, 1⅞" dia. at base. **$125.00 – 150.00.**

Chromium and leather table lighter, made by D.R.P. in Germany. Circa early 1950s. 3¼"h, 4"w. **$60.00 – 75.00.**

Large chromium lift arm table lighter, made by A.T.M. Circa late 1940s. 4⅜"h, 3⅛"w. **$60.00 – 80.00.**

The "Classic Jumbo" large chromium and leather lift arm table lighter, made in England by Brevete S.G.D.C. (has a unique round knob to operate the flint wheel). Circa 1930s. 4⅜"h, 3¼"w. **$140.00 – 175.00.**

Chromium picturesque table lighter, made by Myflam (lights by pushing button on the top of the lighter). Circa late 1940s. 2⅜"h, 3"w. **$40.00 – 60.00.**

Brass with a leather band butane table lighter, made by Sparklet Devices Inc. Circa late 1950s. 4¼"h, 2⅝"w. **$30.00 – 40.00.**

Brass table lighter with a built-in Swiss made Phinney-Walker alarm clock, made by Evans. Circa late 1940s. 5"h, 2⅜" dia. at base. **$125.00 – 150.00.**

The "Flamidor" chromium automatic table lighter, made by Brevete S.G.D.G. in France. Circa mid 1950s. 2⅞"h, 3⅜"w. **$60.00 – 75.00.**

Chromium and wooden butane table lighter, made in Japan. Circa 1970s. 3"h, 2⅛"w. **$10.00 – 15.00.**

Brass lighter with a clear Lucite base, made by Evans (base has a golfer frozen in motion missing the ball). Circa mid 1950s. 3¾"h, 2"w. **$75.00 – 100.00.**

Miscellaneous Tobacco Accessories

Metal cigarette dispenser with slide mechanism in the box to release cigarettes. Circa 1930s. 2½"h, 6"w. **$20.00 – 30.00.**

The Injecto lighter fuel filler, made by Gey Products Corp. Circa late 1940s. 5"h, 3½"w. **$50.00 – 75.00.**

Metal cigar cutter in the shape of a ship's speed indicator, made in Germany. Circa mid 1930s. 5"h, 2¾"w. **$75.00 – 100.00.**

Cigarette lighter fuel dispenser, made by Van Lite. Cost was one cent to fuel lighter. Circa 1950s. 19"h, 7"w. **$300.00 – 350.00.**

Brass match dispenser with built-in cigar cutter at the base. Dispensed boxed wooden matches for one cent a box. Circa 1920s. 13½"h, 5¾"w. **$225.00 – 250.00.**

Miscellaneous Tobacco Accessories

Ceramic red cap train porter. Luggage holds cigarettes and boxed matches with ashtray at the base. Circa 1930s. 7⅞"h, 4¾"w. **$150.00 – 175.00.**

Metal match dispenser. Sold two books of matches for one cent. Circa early 1950s. 14"h, 5"w. **$75.00 – 100.00.**

Ladies' lined, alligator, brass-trimmed handbag made by Evans. The makeup case (made of leather) includes a lighter, cigarette case, comb, lip stick, and compact. The handbag is divided into four open compartments and one compartment with a flap closure, also included is a leather coin purse attached to the inside of the handbag by a chain. Circa 1930s. 9"h, 8"w. **$400.00 – 600.00.**

Zippo figural display of "windy," depicting that Zippo lighters are windproof. Circa 1990s. Figurine, 8¾"h, 4¾"; dome with base, 10¼"h, 6"w. **$200.00 – 250.00.**

Display board with twelve pocket lighters, made by Satelite. Circa 1950s. Display, 10¼"h, 8¼"w; lighters, 1⅛"h, 1⅛"w. **$100.00 – 125.00.**

Miscellaneous Tobacco Accessories

Display board with 12 lighters, made by Jet fuel. Circa 1996. Display, 13¾"h, 8"w; lighters, 2"h, 1¾"w. **$100.00 – 130.00.**

Punch board to try and win cigarettes. Circa mid 1930s. 8¼"h, 9¼"w. **$75.00 – 125.00.**

Retail display board with packages of Ronson wicks. Circa 1950s. Display, 10"h, 10¼"w; packs of wicks, 1½"h, 3¼"w. **$50.00 – 75.00.**

Display with 24 units of flints, made by Five Star. Circa 1950s. Flint cards, 2⅛"h, 1¼"w; display, 10¼"h, 6¾"w. **$10.00 – 20.00.**

Retail display of eight brass and leather lighters, made by Evans. Circa early 1950s. Lighters, 2"h, 1½"w; display, 12⅞"h, 11½"w. **$400.00 – 500.00.**

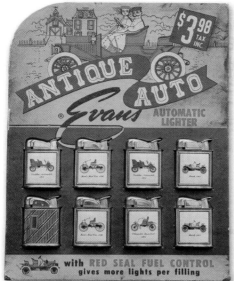

Display with eight "Antique Auto" lighters, made by Evans. Circa early 1950s. Lighters, 2"h, 1½"w; display, 11"h, 8½"w. **$400.00 – 500.00.**

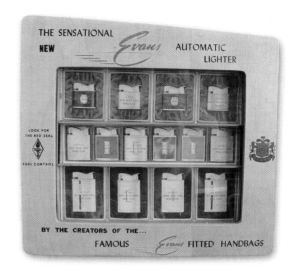

Enamel ladies' compact, made by Evans. Circa early 1930s. ⅜"h, 2⅛"w. **$50.00 – 70.00.**

Wood, glass, and metal store display cabinet for Evans. Holds 14 lighters. Circa mid 1930s. 14"h, 14½"w. **$100.00 – 125.00.**

Metal and imitation pearl and diamond cigarette case/purse, made by Evans. Circa late 1930s. 3¾"h, 3¾"w. **$75.00 – 100.00.**

Miscellaneous Tobacco Accessories

Display board with 12 striker lighters, made by Nesor. Circa 1950. Lighter, 1¾"h, 1⅛"w; display, 10¼"h, 7¼"w. **$75.00 – 100.00.**

Chrome table lighter, made by Ronson, on a retail display for Mother's Day. Circa 1936. Lighter, 2⅜"h, 1¾"w; display, 11¾"h, 9"w. **$75.00 – 100.00.**

Windy lighter with figurine in a dome with a music box as the base, made by Zippo. Circa 1990s. Lighter, 2⅛"h, 1½"w; Windy figurine, 3⅛"h, 1¾"w; dome and music box base, 5½"h, 2⅝"w. **$30.00 – 50.00.**

Metal wrench set, made by Ronson. Circa 1910s. 1½"h, 6"w. **$75.00 – 100.00.**

Wood and metal table cigarette case in the shape of an early gun boat. Circa 1930s. 2"h, 7"w. **$30.00 – 50.00.**

Gold-tone with red jewel compact, made by Evans. Circa mid 1930s. ¾"h, 2½" dia. **$50.00 – 75.00.**

Wooden cigarette box that holds three packs of cigarettes. When lid is opened the cigarettes raise up. Fine detail on the inside of lid. Circa 1930s. 4"h, 4¾"w. **$100.00 – 150.00.**

Miscellaneous Tobacco Accessories

Leather match box, made in Jamaica. Circa 2001. 2¼"h, 1⅝"w. **$5.00 – 10.00.**

Flint kits in the shape of a cigarette lighter, made by Fisher. Circa mid 1950s. 2"h, 1¼"w. **$5.00 – 10.00 each.**

Lighter service kit, made by Ronson. Has instruction booklet, cleaning brush, wick with inserter, flints, and lighter fluid. Circa late 1930s. Box, 2½"h, 6½"w. **$25.00 – 50.00.**

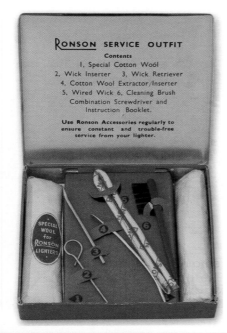

Service outfit made by Ronson. Contains instruction book, wool packing, wick, brush, and miscellaneous tools. Circa 1930s. Box, 3"h, 3½"w. **$25.00 – 50.00.**

Bakelite book cigarette holder, "The Courtship of Lady Nicotine" made by Colt. Also held matches and has an ashtray with a match striker. 6½"h, 5"w. **$400.00 – 500.00.**

"Jiffy Refills," made by Ronson. 6.0cc of lighter fluid packaged in container shaped like a lighter. Circa late 1930s. Fluid, 2¼"h, 1⅛"w; box, 5¾"h, 7⅛"w. **$25.00 – 50.00.**

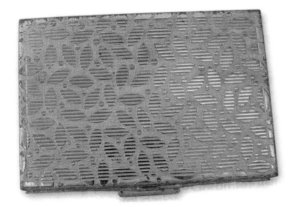

Brass and gold-tone compact, made by Evans. Circa 1930s. 2⅛"h, 3"w. **$60.00 – 75.00.**

Miscellaneous Tobacco Accessories

Brass and enamel ladies' compact, made by Evans. Circa 1930s. 2⅛"h, 3"w. **$70.00 – 90.00.**

A box of one gross of envelopes of wicks with inserters, manufactured by Ronson. Circa mid 1930s. Box, 2½"h, 5"w. **$30.00 – 50.00.**

Colored plastic Christmas tree decoration with a bear sitting on a lit cigarette lighter. Sold at K-Mart stores. Circa 1997. 3"h, 1½"w. **$25.00 – 40.00.**

Tin can of lighter fluid, made by Lito. Circa 1930s. 5¾"h, 2⅞"w. **$15.00 – 20.00.**

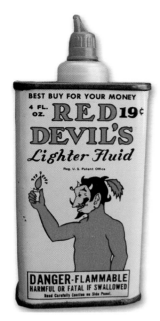

Tin can of lighter fuel, made by Red Devil's. Circa 1940s. 5"h, 2⅛"w. **$15.00 – 20.00.**

From the Old West to the 20th century.

Hand-carved wooden Indians are as popular today as they were in the 1600's when the Native Americans first introduced English settlers to tobacco in Virginia.

Ralph Gallagher along with sons John and Frank bring 3 generations of carving experience to each creation.

The Gallaghers are half Mandan and half Dakota. Ralph was born in an abandoned train car in the south in 1926. He has been carving out 2 of these signed masterpieces a week since 1946.

These hand-crafted Indians were originally created for merchants to display in front of their stores to advertise the sale of tobacco products. Soon they became a symbol of good luck because of soaring tobacco sales since the 1600's.

Good luck is what they have brought to us, and the many other merchants that still display them today.

The Gallaghers hope that the purchase of one of these Indians will bring anyone who purchases one the same good fortune that they have to his family.

The signature series is only available through Pro-Tint. For more information, contact Galen or Kim at (303) 233-7315.

Ralph Gallagher is one of the few carvers in the world that still uses authentic handcrafted tools.

Six foot cigar store Indian carved out of wood and painted by Ralph Gallager. Circa 1990s. **$1,000.00 – 1,500.00.**

Plastic donkey cigarette dispenser. Made in China. Fill the top compartment with cigarettes, press down on the donkey's ears and the tail raises up to dispense the cigarette. Circa 1990s. 5¾"h, 7½"w. **$15.00 – 30.00.**

Miscellaneous Tobacco Accessories

Round metal humidor can that held 50 cigarettes, made by Phillip Morris & Co. Circa 1930s. 3¼"h, 2⅝" dia. **$40.00 – 60.00.**

Cigarette tin, made by Lucky Strike. Circa 1930s. 2⅝"h, 4½"w. **$30.00 – 50.00.**

Cigarette tin, made by Old Gold. Circa 1930s. 3"h, 2¼"w. **$20.00 – 30.00.**

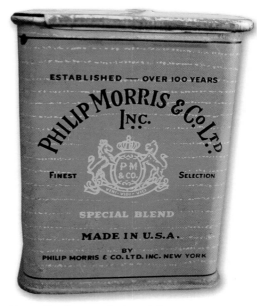

Cigarette tin, made by Phillip Morris & Co. Circa 1930s. 3"h, 2¼"w. **$20.00 – 30.00.**

Old Gold cigarette tin. Circa 1930s. 4⅜"h, 5¾"w.
$25.00 – 40.00.

Camel cigarette tin. Circa 1930s. 4⅜"h,
5¾"w. **$25.00 – 40.00.**

Metal Hennessy cognac bottle table lighter/cigarette
dispenser. Lighter in the lid, bottle pulls apart for
cigarettes, when opened it plays music. Circa mid
1950s. 13½"h, 3" dia. **$60.00 – 80.00.**

Miscellaneous Tobacco Accessories

Chromium butane pocket lighters on a cardboard display, by Bentley. Circa mid 1950s. Lighter, 1½"h, 2"w; display,14⅜"h, 8¾"w. **$125.00 – 150.00.**

Chromium sports model butane pocket lighters on cardboard display by Bentley. Circa late 1950s. Lighter, 1½"h, 2"w; display, 11"h, 9½"w. **$125.00 – 150.00.**

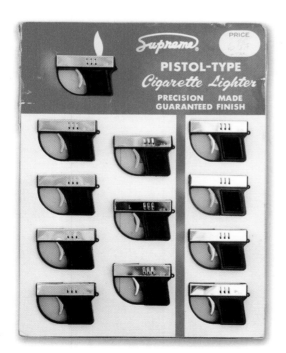

Brass-plated ship's wheel cigarette holder (turn the wheel to raise cigarettes). Circa mid 1950s. 5¼"h, 3⅞" dia. at base. **$30.00 – 40.00.**

Chromium and plastic gun lighters on a display board, made by Supreme. Circa late 1950s. Gun, 1½"h, 2¼"w; display, 12"h, 9"w. **$100.00 – 125.00.**

Penciliters, both made by Havalite. Circa 1950. (a) Chromium and black plastic. 5⅝"h. **$30.00 – 40.00.** (b) Chromium with black and white plastic, 5½"h. **$30.00 – 40.00.**

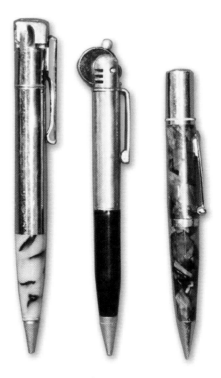

Penciliters. (a) Chromium and Bakelite, made in Occupied Japan. Circa 1949. 5½"h. **$50.00 – 70.00.** (b) Metal and plastic, made by Automet. Circa 1950s. 5⅜"h. **$20.00 – 30.00.** (c) Chromium and plastic, made by LECTRoLITE. Circa late 1940s. 5"h. **$25.00 – 35.00.**

Match safes. (a) Brass. Circa 1900. 2¾"h, 1½"w. **$35.00 – 50.00.** (b) Silver-plated. Circa 1900. 2¾"h, 1½"w. **$40.00 – 60.00.**

Matches and box from Belgium. The box contains a built in snuffer (matches were like candles and could be reused). Circa 1900. 3½"h, 1½"w. **$25.00 – 50.00.**

Miscellaneous Tobacco Accessories

(a) Cigar holder in leather and velvet case. Circa 1920s. 2¼"h, ½" dia. **$30.00 – 40.00.** (b & c) Metal and plastic cigarette holders. Circa early 1950s. 2"h, ⅜" dia. **$10.00 – 15.00 each.**

Metal and enamel art deco cigarette holder. Circa late 1930s. 4½"h, 2⅞" dia. **$20.00 – 30.00.**

Accessories by Ronson. (a) Package of flints, wicks, fuel, and brush. Circa late 1940s. 2"h, 1⅛"w. **$10.00 – 15.00.** (b) Package of five flints. Circa late 1940s. 1½"h, 1"w. **$10.00 – 15.00.**

Flint and wick in individual packs on a cardboard display by Laymon's. Circa late 1930s. Display, 11"h, 10½"w. **$15.00 – 30.00.**

Wooden roll top cigarette box. Circa mid 1930s. 1⅞"h, 3⅜"w. **$30.00 – 50.00.**

Silver match box covers. Both circa late 1920s. (a) 1¾"h, 1¼"w. **$15.00 – 25.00.** (b) 2¼"h, 1½"w. **$15.00 – 25.00 each.**

"Sonny Boy" tin cigarette box from England. Circa mid 1920s. 3"h, 3⅜"w. **$20.00 – 30.00.**

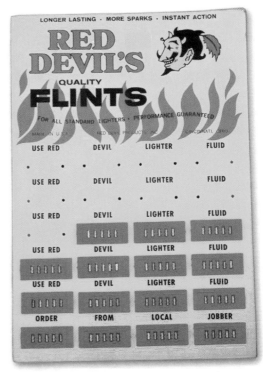

Red Devil's flint display card. Circa 1993. 10¼"h, 6⅞"w. **$.50 each.**

Miscellaneous Tobacco Accessories

Gold-tone mechanical pencil with lighter under the cap, made by Allbright in New York. Circa mid 1950s. 5"h, ½" dia. **$25.00 – 40.00.**

Chromium match box (has a sliding door to remove matches and striker on the bottom). Circa late 1930s. 2"h, 1½"w. **$10.00 – 20.00.**

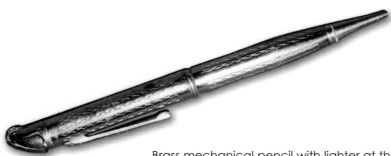

Brass mechanical pencil with lighter at the top, made by Stewart. Circa mid 1950s. 5⅛"h, ⅜"dia. **$25.00 – 40.00.**

Chromium cigarette package holder, made by Dunhill (spring loaded to open for a pack of cigarettes). Circa late 1950s. 3"h, 2¼"w. **$70.00 – 90.00.**

Brass combat shell desk lighter (the 50 caliber shell is a memorable souvenir of W.W. II) with gift box and instructions, a product of Shaw-Barton. Circa late 1940s. 5½"h, ¾" dia. **$30.00 – 50.00.**

Brass and leatherette cigarette holder, made by Amity. Circa late 1950s. 3⅝"h, 2⅜"w. **$5.00 – 10.00.**

Lucky Strike flat cigarette tin. Circa 1940s. 4⅜"h, 5¾"w. **$40.00 – 60.00.**

The "Penciliter" in chromium and green-pearl plastic, made by Ronson. Circa 1934. 5⅝"h, ½" dia. **$90.00 – 115.00.**

Miscellaneous Tobacco Accessories

Plastic roll top cigarette dispenser with leather on the sides, made by Rolinx in England. Circa 1952. 2⅜"h, 5¾"w. **$30.00 – 40.00.**

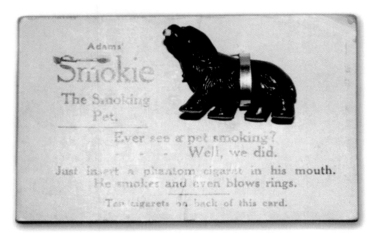

"Smokie the Smoking Pet," made by Adams (came with ten cigarettes and the dog could blow smoke rings). Circa 1950s. Dog, 1"h, 1½"w; display, 2¼"h, 3⅝"w. **$30.00 – 50.00.**

Chromium "Penciliter," made by Ronson. Circa 1948. 5⅜"h, ½" dia. **$60.00 – 85.00.**

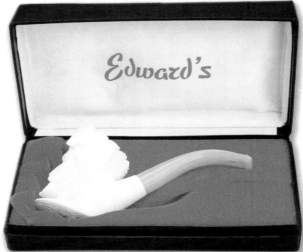

Meerschaum pipe (turns red after many years of smoking), made by Edward's Pipe Shop in Englewood, Colorado. Circa late 1960s. 3¼"h, 4¾"w. **$100.00 – 150.00.**

Oriental wooden roll top box (when top is rolled back, the mechanism dispenses a cigarette), made in Japan. Circa 1930s. 2⅞"h, 4⅞"w. **$85.00 – 110.00.**

Painted wooden bird cigarette dispenser, made in Japan. Circa 1930s. 4½"h, 7½"w. **$85.00 – 110.00.**

The bird picks up a cigarette in its beak, out of the sliding compartment, when the lever by its feet is moved downward.

Miscellaneous Tobacco Accessories

Advertising book of matches and mechanical pencil (pencil has a small truck in the clear end that moves back and forth), for Walt Flanagan & Co in Denver, Colorado. Circa 1950s. Matches, **$3.00 – 5.00**; pencil, **$20.00 – 30.00.**

Brass pipe and match holder (matches are held inside the boot), made by Trophy Craft. Circa early 1940s. 3⅞"h, 3¾"w. **$20.00 – 40.00.**

Salem promotional gift (try to get the cigarettes in the pack). Circa 1950s. ½"h, 3⅞" dia. **$20.00 – 30.00.**

Ceramic pipe holder. Circa 1960s. 4¾"h, 3⅝"w. **$25.00 – 35.00.**

Bellhop shown with black luggage for cigarettes and match box. Circa mid 1930s. 6"h, 3⅜"w at base. **$75.00 – 100.00.**

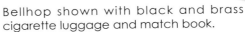

Bellhop shown with black and brass cigarette luggage and match book.

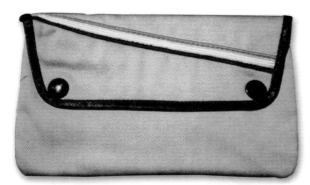

Canvas tobacco pouch with red, white, and blue stripes on the flap. Circa 1942. 3¾"h, 6"w. **$15.00 – 20.00.**

Lighter fluid tin for cigar lighters, can had a cork stopper made by Enoz. Circa early 1920s. 3¾" h, 2¼"w. **$20.00 – 30.00.**

Brass cigarette caddy with a raised design in the center of the lid and a wooden handle, made by Park Sherman. Circa 1940s. 1¼"h, 3½"w. **$10.00 – 20.00.**

COLLECTOR BOOKS
informing today's collector

www.collectorbooks.com

For over two decades we have been keeping collectors informed on trends and values in all fields of antiques and collectibles.

DOLLS, FIGURES & TEDDY BEARS

6315 **American Character Dolls**, Izen $24.95
6317 **Arranbee Dolls**, The Dolls that Sell on Sight, DeMillar/Brevik $24.95
2079 **Barbie Doll** Fashion, Volume I, Eames $24.95
4846 **Barbie Doll** Fashion, Volume II, Eames $24.95
6319 **Barbie Doll** Fashion, Volume III, Eames $29.95
6022 The **Barbie Doll** Years, 5th Ed., Olds $19.95
5352 Collector's Ency. of **Barbie** Doll Exclusives & More, 2nd Ed., Augustyniak .$24.95
5904 Collector's Guide to **Celebrity Dolls**, Spurgeon $24.95
5599 Collector's Guide to **Dolls of the 1960s and 1970s**, Sabulis $24.95
6030 Collector's Guide to **Horsman Dolls**, Jensen $29.95
6224 **Doll Values**, Antique to Modern, 7th Ed., Moyer.....................$12.95
6033 **Modern Collectible Dolls**, Volume VI, Moyer $24.95
5689 **Nippon Dolls** & Playthings, Van Patten/Lau $29.95
5365 **Peanuts Collectibles**, Podley/Bang $24.95
6336 Official **Precious Moments** Collector's Guide to Company **Dolls**, Bomm ...$19.95
6026 **Small Dolls of the 40s & 50s**, Stover $29.95
5253 Story of **Barbie**, 2nd Ed., Westenhouser $24.95
5277 **Talking Toys** of the 20th Century, Lewis $15.95
2084 **Teddy Bears**, Annalee's & **Steiff** Animals, 3rd Series, Mandel $19.95
4880 World of **Raggedy Ann** Collectibles, Avery $24.95

TOYS & MARBLES

2333 Antique & Collectible **Marbles**, 3rd Ed., Grist $9.95
5900 Collector's Guide to **Battery Toys**, 2nd Edition, Hultzman $24.95
4566 Collector's Guide to **Tootsietoys**, 2nd Ed., Richter $19.95
5169 Collector's Guide to **TV Toys** & Memorabilia, 2nd Ed., Davis/Morgan $24.95
5593 Grist's Big Book of **Marbles**, 2nd Ed. $24.95
3970 Grist's Machine-Made & Contemporary **Marbles**, 2nd Ed. $9.95
6128 **Hot Wheels**, The Ultimate Redline Guide, 1968 – 1977, Clark/Wicker $24.95
5830 **McDonald's** Collectibles, 2nd Edition, Henriques/DuVall $24.95
1540 Modern **Toys**, 1930–1980, Baker $19.95
6237 **Rubber Toy Vehicles**, Leopard $19.95
6340 **Schroeder's Collectible Toys**, Antique to Modern Price Guide, 9th Ed. $17.95
5908 **Toy Car** Collector's Guide, Johnson $19.95

FURNITURE

3716 American **Oak** Furniture, Book II, McNerney $12.95
1118 Antique **Oak** Furniture, Hill $7.95
3720 Collector's Encyclopedia of **American** Furniture, Vol. III, Swedberg $24.95
5359 Early **American** Furniture, Obbard $12.95
3906 **Heywood-Wakefield** Modern Furniture, Rouland $18.95
6338 **Roycroft** Furniture & Collectibles, Koon $24.95
6343 **Stickley Brothers** Furniture, Koon $24.95
1885 **Victorian** Furniture, Our American Heritage, McNerney $9.95
3829 **Victorian** Furniture, Our American Heritage, Book II, McNerney $9.95

JEWELRY, HATPINS, WATCHES & PURSES

4704 Antique & Collectible **Buttons**, Wisniewski $19.95
6323 **Christmas Pins**, Past & Present, 2nd Edition, Gallina $19.95
4850 Collectible **Costume Jewelry**, Simonds $24.95
5675 Collectible **Silver Jewelry**, Rezazadeh $24.95
3722 Collector's Ency. of **Compacts**, Carryalls & Face Powder Boxes, Mueller ...$24.95
4940 **Costume Jewelry**, A Practical Handbook & Value Guide, Rezazadeh $24.95
5812 Fifty Years of Collectible **Fashion Jewelry**, 1925 – 1975, Baker $24.95
6330 **Handkerchiefs**: A Collector's Guide, Guarnaccia/Guggenheim .$24.95
1424 **Hatpins** & Hatpin Holders, Baker $9.95
5695 **Ladies' Vintage Accessories**, Bruton $24.95

1181 100 Years of Collectible **Jewelry**, 1850 – 1950, Baker $9.95
6337 **Purse Masterpieces**, Schwartz $29.95
4729 **Sewing Tools** & Trinkets, Thompson $24.95
6038 **Sewing Tools** & Trinkets, Volume 2, Thompson $24.95
6039 Signed Beauties of **Costume Jewelry**, Brown $24.95
6341 Signed Beauties of **Costume Jewelry**, Volume II, Brown $24.95
5620 Unsigned Beauties of **Costume Jewelry**, Brown $24.95
4878 Vintage & Contemporary **Purse Accessories**, Gerson $24.95
5696 Vintage & Vogue Ladies' **Compacts**, 2nd Edition, Gerson $29.95
5923 **Vintage Jewelry** for Investment & Casual Wear, Edeen $24.95

ARTIFACTS, GUNS, KNIVES, TOOLS, PRIMITIVES

6021 **Arrowheads** of the Central Great Plains, Fox $19.95
1868 Antique **Tools**, Our American Heritage, McNerney $9.95
5616 Big Book of **Pocket Knives**, Stewart $19.95
4943 Field Gde. to Flint **Arrowheads** & **Knives** of the N. American Indian, Tully ...$9.95
3885 **Indian Artifacts** of the Midwest, Book II, Hothem $16.95
4870 **Indian Artifacts** of the Midwest, Book III, Hothem $18.95
5685 **Indian Artifacts** of the Midwest, Book IV, Hothem $19.95
6132 **Modern Guns**, Identification & Values, 14th Ed., Quertermous $14.95
2164 **Primitives**, Our American Heritage, McNerney $9.95
1759 **Primitives**, Our American Heritage, 2nd Series, McNerney $14.95
6031 Standard **Knife** Collector's Guide, 4th Ed., Ritchie & Stewart $14.95
5999 **Wilderness Survivor's Guide**, Hamper $12.95

PAPER COLLECTIBLES & BOOKS

5902 **Boys' & Girls' Book** Series, Jones $19.95
5153 Collector's Guide to **Children's Books**, 1850 to 1950, Volume II, Jones $19.95
1441 Collector's Guide to **Post Cards**, Wood $9.95
5926 **Duck Stamps**, Chappell $9.95
2081 Guide to Collecting **Cookbooks**, Allen $14.95
2080 Price Guide to **Cookbooks** & Recipe Leaflets, Dickinson $9.95
3973 **Sheet Music** Reference & Price Guide, 2nd Ed., Pafik & Guiheen $19.95
6041 Vintage **Postcards** for the Holidays, Reed $24.95

GLASSWARE

5602 Anchor Hocking's **Fire-King** & More, 2nd Ed. $24.95
6321 **Carnival Glass**, The Best of the Best, Edwards/Carwile $29.95
5823 **Collectible Glass Shoes**, 2nd Edition, Wheatley $24.95
6325 Coll. **Glassware from the 40s, 50s & 60s**, 7th Ed., Florence $19.95
1810 Collector's Encyclopedia of **American Art Glass**, Shuman $29.95
6327 Collector's Encyclopedia of **Depression Glass**, 16th Ed., Florence $19.95
1961 Collector's Encyclopedia of **Fry Glassware**, Fry Glass Society $24.95
1664 Collector's Encyclopedia of **Heisey Glass**, 1925 – 1938, Bredehoft $24.95
3905 Collector's Encyclopedia of **Milk Glass**, Newbound $24.95
5820 Collector's Guide to **Glass Banks**, Reynolds $24.95
6454 **Crackle Glass** From Around the World, Weitman $24.95
6125 **Elegant Glassware** of the Depression Era, 10th Ed., Florence $24.95
6334 Encyclopedia of **Paden City Glass**, Domitz $24.95
3981 Evers' Standard **Cut Glass** Value Guide $12.95
6462 Florence's **Glass Kitchen Shakers**, 1930 – 1950s $19.95
5042 Florence's **Glassware Pattern Identification** Guide, Vol. I $18.95
5615 Florence's **Glassware Pattern Identification** Guide, Vol. II $19.95
6142 Florence's **Glassware Pattern Identification** Guide, Vol. III $19.95
4719 **Fostoria**, Etched, Carved & Cut Designs, Vol. II, Kerr $24.95
6226 **Fostoria** Value Guide, Long/Seate $19.95
5899 **Glass & Ceramic Baskets**, White $19.95
6460 **Glass Animals**, Second Edition, Spencer $24.95

6127	The **Glass Candlestick** Book, Volume 1, Akro Agate to Fenton, Felt/Stoer	$24.95
6228	The **Glass Candlestick** Book, Volume 2, Fostoria to Jefferson, Felt/Stoer	$24.95
6461	The **Glass Candlestick** Book, Volume 3, Kanawha to Wright, Felt/Stoer	$29.95
6329	**Glass Tumblers**, 1860s to 1920s, Bredehoft	$29.95
4644	Imperial **Carnival Glass**, Burns	$18.95
5827	**Kitchen Glassware** of the Depression Years, 6th Ed., Florence	$24.95
5600	Much More Early American **Pattern Glass**, Metz	$17.95
6133	**Mt. Washington Art Glass**, Sisk	$49.95
6136	Pocket Guide to **Depression Glass** & More, 13th Ed., Florence	$12.95
6448	Standard Encyclopedia of **Carnival Glass**, 9th Ed., Edwards/Carwile	$29.95
6449	Standard **Carnival Glass** Price Guide, 14th Ed., Edwards/Carwile	$9.95
6035	Standard Encyclopedia of **Opalescent Glass**, 4th Ed., Edwards/Carwile	$24.95
6241	Treasures of **Very Rare Depression Glass**, Florence	$39.95

POTTERY

4929	**American Art Pottery**, Sigafoose	$24.95
1312	**Blue & White Stoneware**, McNerney	$9.95
4851	Collectible **Cups & Saucers**, Harran	$18.95
6326	Collectible **Cups & Saucers**, Book III, Harran	$24.95
6344	Collectible **Vernon Kilns**, 2nd Edition, Nelson	$29.95
6331	Collecting **Head Vases**, Barron	$24.95
1373	Collector's Encyclopedia of **American Dinnerware**, Cunningham	$24.95
4931	Collector's Encyclopedia of **Bauer Pottery**, Chipman	$24.95
5034	Collector's Encyclopedia of **California Pottery**, 2nd Ed., Chipman	$24.95
3723	Collector's Encyclopedia of **Cookie Jars**, Book II, Roerig	$24.95
4939	Collector's Encyclopedia of **Cookie Jars**, Book III, Roerig	$24.95
5748	Collector's Encyclopedia of **Fiesta**, 9th Ed., Huxford	$24.95
3961	Collector's Encyclopedia of **Early Noritake**, Alden	$24.95
3812	Collector's Encyclopedia of **Flow Blue China**, 2nd Ed., Gaston	$24.95
3431	Collector's Encyclopedia of **Homer Laughlin China**, Jasper	$24.95
1276	Collector's Encyclopedia of **Hull Pottery**, Roberts	$19.95
5609	Collector's Encyclopedia of **Limoges Porcelain**, 3rd Ed., Gaston	$29.95
2334	Collector's Encyclopedia of **Majolica Pottery**, Katz-Marks	$19.95
1358	Collector's Encyclopedia of **McCoy Pottery**, Huxford	$19.95
5677	Collector's Encyclopedia of **Niloak**, 2nd Edition, Gifford	$29.95
5564	Collector's Encyclopedia of **Pickard China**, Reed	$29.95
5679	Collector's Encyclopedia of **Red Wing Art Pottery**, Dollen	$24.95
5618	Collector's Encyclopedia of **Rosemeade Pottery**, Dommel	$24.95
5841	Collector's Encyclopedia of **Roseville Pottery**, Revised, Huxford/Nickel	$24.95
5842	Collector's Encyclopedia of **Roseville Pottery**, 2nd Series, Huxford/Nickel	$24.95
5917	Collector's Encyclopedia of **Russel Wright**, 3rd Editon, Kerr	$29.95
5921	Collector's Encyclopedia of **Stangl Artware**, Lamps, and Birds, Runge	$29.95
3314	Collector's Encyclopedia of **Van Briggle Art Pottery**, Sasicki	$24.95
5680	Collector's Guide to **Feather Edge Ware**, McAllister	$19.95
6124	Collector's Guide to **Made in Japan Ceramics**, Book IV, White	$24.95
1425	**Cookie Jars**, Westfall	$9.95
3440	**Cookie Jars**, Book II, Westfall	$19.95
6316	Decorative **American Pottery & Whiteware**, Wilby	$29.95
5909	**Dresden Porcelain** Studios, Harran	$29.95
5918	Florence's Big Book of **Salt & Pepper Shakers**	$24.95
6320	Gaston's **Blue Willow**, 3rd Edition	$19.95
2379	Lehner's Ency. of **U.S. Marks** on Pottery, Porcelain & China	$24.95
4722	**McCoy Pottery**, Collector's Reference & Value Guide, Hanson/Nissen	$19.95
5913	**McCoy Pottery**, Volume III, Hanson & Nissen	$24.95
6333	**McCoy Pottery Wall Pockets** & Decorations, Nissen	$24.95
6135	**North Carolina Art Pottery**, 1900 – 1960, James/Leftwich	$24.95
6335	Pictorial Guide to **Pottery & Porcelain Marks**, Lage	$29.95
5691	**Post86 Fiesta**, Identification & Value Guide, Racheter	$19.95
1670	**Red Wing Collectibles**, DePasquale	$9.95
1440	**Red Wing Stoneware**, DePasquale	$9.95

6037	**Rookwood Pottery**, Nicholson & Thomas	$24.95
6236	**Rookwood Pottery**, 10 Years of Auction Results, 1990 – 2002, Treadway	$39.95
1632	**Salt & Pepper Shakers**, Guarnaccia	$9.95
5091	**Salt & Pepper Shakers** II, Guarnaccia	$18.95
3443	**Salt & Pepper Shakers** IV, Guarnaccia	$18.95
3738	**Shawnee Pottery**, Mangus	$24.95
4629	Turn of the Century **American Dinnerware**, 1880s–1920s, Jasper	$24.95
5924	**Zanesville Stoneware** Company, Rans, Ralston & Russell	$24.95

OTHER COLLECTIBLES

5916	Advertising **Paperweights**, Holiner & Kammerman	$24.95
5838	Advertising **Thermometers**, Merritt	$16.95
5898	Antique & Contemporary **Advertising Memorabilia**, Summers	$24.95
5814	Antique **Brass & Copper** Collectibles, Gaston	$24.95
1880	Antique **Iron**, McNerney	$9.95
3872	Antique **Tins**, Dodge	$24.95
4845	Antique **Typewriters & Office Collectibles**, Rehr	$19.95
5607	Antiquing and Collecting on the **Internet**, Parry	$12.95
1128	**Bottle** Pricing Guide, 3rd Ed., Cleveland	$7.95
6345	**Business & Tax Guide** for Antiques & Collectibles, Kelly	$14.95
6225	Captain John's **Fishing Tackle** Price Guide, Kolbeck/Lewis	$19.95
3718	Collectible **Aluminum**, Grist	$16.95
6342	Collectible **Soda Pop** Memorabilia, Summers	$24.95
5060	Collectible **Souvenir Spoons**, Bednersh	$19.95
5676	Collectible **Souvenir Spoons**, Book II, Bednersh	$29.95
5666	Collector's Encyclopedia of **Granite Ware**, Book 2, Greguire	$29.95
5836	Collector's Guide to **Antique Radios**, 5th Ed., Bunis	$19.95
3966	Collector's Guide to **Inkwells**, Identification & Values, Badders	$18.95
4947	Collector's Guide to **Inkwells**, Book II, Badders	$19.95
5681	Collector's Guide to **Lunchboxes**, White	$19.95
4864	Collector's Guide to **Wallace Nutting Pictures**, Ivankovich	$18.95
5683	**Fishing Lure** Collectibles, Vol. 1, Murphy/Edmisten	$29.95
6328	**Flea Market Trader**, 14th Ed., Huxford	$12.95
6227	**Garage Sale** & Flea Market Annual, 11th Edition, Huxford	$19.95
4945	**G-Men and FBI Toys** and Collectibles, Whitworth	$18.95
3819	**General Store** Collectibles, Wilson	$24.95
5912	The **Heddon** Legacy, A Century of Classic **Lures**, Roberts & Pavey	$29.95
2216	**Kitchen Antiques**, 1790–1940, McNerney	$14.95
5991	**Lighting Devices** & Accessories of the 17th – 19th Centuries, Hamper	$9.95
5686	**Lighting Fixtures** of the Depression Era, Book I, Thomas	$24.95
4950	The **Lone Ranger**, Collector's Reference & Value Guide, Felbinger	$18.95
6028	Modern **Fishing Lure** Collectibles, Vol. 1, Lewis	$24.95
6131	Modern **Fishing Lure** Collectibles, Vol. 2, Lewis	$24.95
6322	Pictorial Guide to **Christmas Ornaments** & Collectibles, Johnson	$29.95
2026	**Railroad** Collectibles, 4th Ed., Baker	$14.95
5619	**Roy Rogers and Dale Evans** Toys & Memorabilia, Coyle	$24.95
6339	**Schroeder's Antiques** Price Guide, 22nd Edition	$14.95
5007	**Silverplated Flatware**, Revised 4th Edition, Hagan	$18.95
6239	**Star Wars** Super Collector's Wish Book, 2nd Ed., Carlton	$29.95
6139	Summers' Guide to **Coca-Cola**, 4th Ed.	$24.95
6324	Summers' Pocket Guide to **Coca-Cola**, 4th Ed.	$12.95
3977	Value Guide to **Gas Station Memorabilia**, Summers & Priddy	$24.95
4877	Vintage **Bar Ware**, Visakay	$24.95
5925	The Vintage Era of **Golf Club Collectibles**, John	$29.95
6010	The Vintage Era of **Golf Club Collectibles** Collector's Log, John	$9.95
6036	Vintage **Quilts**, Aug, Newman & Roy	$24.95
4935	The W.F. Cody **Buffalo Bill** Collector's Guide with Values	$24.95

This is only a partial listing of the books on antiques that are available from Collector Books. All books are well illustrated and contain current values. Most of these books are available from your local bookseller, antique dealer, or public library. If you are unable to locate certain titles in your area, you may order by mail from **COLLECTOR BOOKS**, P.O. Box 3009, Paducah, KY 42002-3009. Customers with Visa, Master Card, or Discover may phone in orders from 7:00a.m. to 5:00 p.m. CT, Monday – Friday, toll free **1-800-626-5420**, or online at **www.collectorbooks.com**. Add $3.00 for postage for the first book ordered and 50¢ for each additional book. Include item number, title, and price when ordering. Allow 14 to 21 days for delivery.

1-800-626-5420   Fax: 1-270-898-8890

www.collectorbooks.com

Schroeder's ANTIQUES Price Guide

...is the #1 bestselling antiques & collectibles value guide on the market today, and here's why...

• More than 400 advisors, well-known dealers, and top-notch collectors work together with our editors to bring you accurate information regarding pricing and identification.

• More than 50,000 items in over 500 categories are listed along with hundreds of sharp original photos that illustrate not only the rare and unusual, but the common, popular collectibles as well.

• Each large close-up shot shows important details clearly. Every subject is represented with histories and background information, a feature not found in any of our competitors' publications.

• Our editors keep abreast of newly developing trends, often adding several new categories a year as the need arises.

8½" x 11" • 608 pages • $14.95

Without doubt, you'll find

Schroeder's Antiques Price Guide

the only one to buy for reliable information and values.

If it merits the interest of today's collector, you'll find it in *Schroeder's*. And you can feel confident that the information we publish is up-to-date and accurate. Our advisors thoroughly check each category to spot inconsistencies, listings that may not be entirely reflective of market dealings, and lines too vague to be of merit. Only the best of the lot remains for publication.

COLLECTOR BOOKS
P.O. Box 3009, Paducah, KY 42002–3009
1-800-626-5420
www.collectorbooks.com